MW01251277

Tainted Love

Tainted Love

WHY YOUR EX IS MAKING YOU MISERABLE AND WHAT YOU CAN DO ABOUT IT

A 28 DAY PLAN

Dr. Julie Gowthorpe, R.S.W.

BALBOA
PRESS

A DIVISION OF HAY HOUSE

ISBN: 978-1-4525-5262-0 (sc)
ISBN: 978-1-4525-5263-7 (hc)
ISBN: 978-1-4525-5261-3 (e)

Library of Congress Control Number: 2012909181

Balboa Press books may be ordered through booksellers or by contacting:
Balboa Press
A Division of Hay House
1663 Liberty Drive
Bloomington, IN 47403
www.balboapress.com
1-(877) 407-4847

Because of the dynamic nature of the Internet, any web addresses or links contained in
this book may have changed since publication and may no longer be valid. The views
expressed in this work are solely those of the author and do not necessarily reflect the
views of the publisher, and the publisher hereby disclaims any responsibility for them.

The author of this book does not dispense medical advice or prescribe the use
of any technique as a form of treatment for physical, emotional, or medical
problems without the advice of a physician, either directly or indirectly. The
intent of the author is only to offer information of a general nature to help you
in your quest for emotional and spiritual well-being. In the event you use any
of the information in this book for yourself, which is your constitutional right,
the author and the publisher assume no responsibility for your actions.

Printed in the United States of America

Balboa Press rev. date: 8/6/2012

Contents

Preface: When Love Goes Wrong

Whether you separated recently or divorced several years ago, a problematic relationship with an ex-spouse can make life miserable. You may share children with your ex, which makes this relationship with your former husband or wife necessary. If you have kids, you likely feel locked in your parenting relationship with your ex and want it to be better. Your couple relationship has ended, but you remain bound as parents. As you probably now realize, the parenting relationship is undivorceable!

First, whether you are a parent or not, divorce does not need to be a bad thing. You may have been unable to continue in your marriage without completely losing yourself. You may have needed to separate from a very toxic situation. Without doubt, life after divorce can be better than life in a miserable marriage. When I grew up in the seventies, life didn't seem so complicated. Except for my friend, Alec, who lived with his mom and step-dad and visited his *real* father sometimes, my world was made up of friends who lived with two heterosexual parents in single family homes. Unlike my children, most of us had the same last name as both of our parents and many of us had mothers who weren't employed outside of the home. Yes, life *seemed* simple. As an adult, however, and a professional who spends most of my time working with divorced parents, I now wonder what was actually going on in some of the seemingly simple, traditional nuclear family, homes. Academics and researchers tell us that nearly half of marriages end in divorce which leaves me questioning, how happy were all those couples I knew as a child? Had the society of my childhood been more accepting of divorce, would many of those parents been happier living separately? How many of my friends would have been happier had their parents decided to live separately?

So, here we are today. We have options. If we are not happy in our marriage, society tells us that we can leave. In fact, we are told that our kids will be happier if they have two happy parents living apart, rather than two unhappy parents living together. You, or your ex-partner, or both of you, decided that you would take that option. You wanted to be happier. I get it. I'm here to help. I also understand that, despite your best intentions, this may not be how things turned out. Whether you are overwhelmed with divorce problems today or are preparing yourself for issues that may unfold, you have decided to take control of the situation with your former partner. This is not an easy decision. You may have been married or in a relationship for several years and have become accustomed to a certain dynamic between you and your ex. Or you may have divorced many years ago but are still having problems with a relationship that you thought you were leaving behind. You may even wonder, *If I try to make changes, do I risk making the situation worse?*

As a psychotherapist who specializes in divorce, I can assure you that, with my help, you can make this better. One of my youngest clients, Nathaniel, a seven-year-old child of parental divorce, calls me his "Talk Doctor." Nathaniel came to see me because his parents were unable to agree on custody and access issues, and Nathaniel was having difficulty coping. Once an extroverted, social child, his mother reported that Nathaniel had become anxious at school, was worried about seemingly minor issues, and would not leave the home for play dates or activities with other children. He frequently complained of stomach pain and headaches. Nathaniel had been examined medically and concerns were attributed to stress. As a professional who has researched the effects of parental conflict on children, this was not a surprise. Nathaniel was clearly exhibiting anxiety related to parental conflict after divorce.

Nathaniel has now been my client for several months and has made significant progress. Nathaniel loves to talk and play. He has articulated his worry that his parents are sad. Nathaniel told me about his efforts to make his parents feel better. He keeps his mom company when she is sad and listens to his dad when his dad is worried about not having enough money. Session by session, Nathaniel has learned that it is not his job to make his parents feel better. His responsibility is to be a kid! Through therapy, Nathaniel has learned how to express feelings so that he does not hold them in and feel worried. He has learned to self-soothe by finding things to do that make him feel better. He has reduced his anxiety to a level where he is happy at school, and he now attends play dates and birthday parties with friends. His parents have also learned that they must shield Nathaniel from their differences in opinion and their concerns.

When I see Nathaniel today, he presents as an articulate, vibrant child who loves his family, pets, and friends. He is always happy to see me. When Nathaniel arrives at my office for appointments, his demeanor reminds me each and every time about how important it is for parents to be happy after divorce. When Nathaniel's parents are happy, Nathaniel is relaxed. When his parents are in conflict, Nathaniel is anxious. As Nathaniel's "Talk Doctor," my job is to help him feel better. Despite the progress Nathaniel has made, he is still vulnerable to any conflict or unhappiness he senses from his parents.

Because of Nathaniel and children in similar circumstances, I have focused great attention, both clinically and in my research, to exploring and learning about the relationship between ex-partners following divorce. Divorced parents deserve to be happy and healthy. Kids are entitled to happiness despite parental divorce. I believe that a comprehensive plan based upon knowledge and action can grant this happiness. As the childhood action hero GI Joe stated so eloquently, "Knowing is half the battle." As a psychotherapist, I believe the other half is to *take this knowledge and do things differently.*

Introduction: Baby, It Ain't Over ... Till the Kids Grow Up and Move Away

The presumably once loving relationship you shared with your ex has deteriorated. Maybe one of you wishes that the relationship had improved and you could still be a couple parenting your child together. Feelings are very complicated in relationships between exes because of the underlying lack of trust; hurt; anger; and, for some, a desire to keep the relationship going even when it is toxic. If you didn't share a child, you could walk away—even run away! Because the parenting relationship continues, the negative feelings that you are experiencing need to improve. Here's an analogy: If you have ever overindulged the night before and awakened to a hangover, you know that eventually the symptoms of consuming too much alcohol will subside. You know that the pounding headache will go away, the nausea will improve, and you will get on with your morning ... or afternoon. The hangover will resolve itself, and you will be okay again. Rationally, you know that the symptoms you are experiencing are simply the consequence of drinking too much, a logical outcome for your choices.

Too much alcohol = dehydration/nausea = a hangover.

Simple, right?

The problem is, you woke up this morning with a headache, body aches, and even some nausea. Your symptoms have nothing to do with drinking too much, eating too much, or overdoing anything. In fact, you are doing your best to be the healthiest you can be. You may be eating right, exercising, and following a regular routine. So why are you feeling so terrible?

You've separated from your ex, maybe even finalized your divorce. You thought things would be better. After all, you're doing your best not to interfere in his[1] new life. You may be doing your best to not question how he spends time with the kids. You may actually like residing separately from your ex—no more worries about tension at home. Work is going well, and you've been socializing with friends. You've empowered yourself with the ten best divorce tunes you could find for your daily runs on the treadmill. Regrettably, despite all the "betters," the impact of not getting along with your ex is wearing on you. Day after day, you still aren't getting along with him. He still can't stand to be around you. You know this conflict isn't good for you or your kids, yet there seems to be no solution. That's what you're feeling—no solution. That's what you wake up to—no solution.

Problems parenting with your ex = headache/nausea = divorce hangover.

Simple, right?

Your headache, or how badly you are feeling, is symptomatic of parenting with someone you don't get along with. You've been arguing—or, as the lawyers call it, *in dispute*—since you ended your couple relationship, and it does not seem to be getting better. You were not naive. You knew that divorce has consequences,

---

1   The pronoun "he" is used throughout the text for clarity purposes only. There is no bias toward either gender or sexual orientation. "He" refers to your husband, your wife, or your partner.

particularly for parents. That was no surprise. You knew that the symptoms of a relationship breakup could include hard feelings, financial strain, and difficult conversations. You assumed that things would be rough for a while and then get better. You may be surprised by the extent of the difficulty you are experiencing and struggling with the lack of improvement. It's like experiencing a hangover without hope—that is, a divorce hangover.

You've tried to be hopeful. You've sought help, talked to your lawyer (many times, according to your itemized legal costs), and met with a therapist. Still, you don't feel well. In fact, at times you feel absolutely terrible. Despite the passing of time, part of you simply wants your family back, not because you truly wish to reunite with your former spouse, but because *parenting apart* is really not working for you. It's worse than you could ever have anticipated. You can't get along with your former spouse under these circumstances no matter how hard you try. It's not like you can wave a wand and make this better. Unlike the headache that was effectively treated with Advil or fluids, the discomfort that accompanies separation from your spouse is not going away.

It's time to try something new. There is a remedy for what you are experiencing, and it starts with you. Starting from the inside, rather than looking out, is not an easy task. Welcome to the little workbook with a strong right hook. Follow this process and you'll feel better and happier than you do today, despite your ex. When you start from the inside, you have the power to change the situation. No longer will you hand your happiness over to someone who seeks to make you unhappy.

Although we are here to talk about divorce, this way of approaching problems (and yes, when you don't get along with your ex, you have a problem) can apply to many areas of life. Every person, married or single, young or old, has experienced a situation where it seemed someone or something was causing him or her to be unhappy. We learn from these experiences. Take Jake, now sixty years young, married thirty-five years this past December to his beautiful wife Linda. The two have three wonderful adult children and a total of seven grandchildren. Jake is happy with his family life. He is happy in his marriage. Jake's problem lies in his relationship with his neighbor. Until three years ago, Jake loved where he lived; his home; and most of all, his view of the lake from his kitchen window. Unfortunately for Jake, when his neighbor Norm inherited a substantial sum of money, how he chose to spend his money began to negatively affect Jake.

Over a three-year period, Norm built several additions on his home, increasing the size of the residence from 1,800 square feet to over 5,000 square feet. With the increased size of the home came a decreased view of the lake for Jake. Consequently, the prized view of the lake from the kitchen window vanished, leaving Jake with only a partial view from his upstairs bathroom. Decorated with an oversized pool, a mega-sized trampoline, and an all-terrain vehicle that verifiably broke neighborhood noise bylaws, the neighbor's home became a gathering place for boundless visitors.

Jake was frustrated. From his perspective, his neighbor had ruined his happiness. Each day, Jake woke up anticipating how his neighbor was going to ruin his day. He felt powerless. Jake tried to ignore Norm and the activity at Norm's home. Regrettably, in the same way you can't ignore your child's other parent, Jake could not ignore his neighbor. Just as you can't move to the other side of the planet to escape your ex, Jake could not move to another city. So what could Jake do? What can you do? Jake had already talked with his neighbor. He explained his feelings—both politely and then less so. From Jake's perspective, following his effort to communicate, his neighbor became more difficult. Norm then purchased a twenty-two-foot camping trailer, which he parked in the driveway. Jake felt hopeless.

Jake's wife, Linda, expressed worry that he was damaging his health by obsessing over Norm's behavior, and she encouraged him to seek help. Linda booked a joint appointment for her and Jake. Through therapy, Jake came to the realization that he could not change his neighbor's behavior. He conquered the first part of the problem by accepting things he could not change, such as the behavior of others. He decided that he would stop investing energy into a relationship that was making him unhappy. Jake realized he had control over how he would enjoy his days and free time. By obsessing less over Norm, Jake found that he had time and energy to focus on things that made him happy. Jake began to make plans with Linda, he scheduled golfing and fishing dates with old friends, and he began to volunteer at a nearby community center. Within a short period of time, Jake began to feel better. He decided to completely change his response to his neighbor—to change the dynamic. For example, Jake purposefully waved at Norm when he was outside, shouted "hello" when he was in his backyard, and even attended a community barbecue and pool party at Norm's home. Jake stopped letting Norm bother him by consciously stepping out of the conflict. With no behavioral change from Norm, Jake disengaged from this toxic dynamic.

One day, Jake looked out and the trailer was gone, allowing him to see the lake from his front yard. Two of Norm's teenagers went off to college, and the trampoline was disassembled. Yes, the house next door was still massive in size, but it no longer mattered. Jake enjoyed being at home with his family. He enjoyed spending his free time doing things that made him feel happy. No one had the power to ruin his happiness, even someone who lived as close as a neighbor.

I was Jake's therapist. He no longer comes to see me because he is too busy enjoying his recent retirement. You are like Jake—two people with different problems but the same solution. I want you to be too busy to worry about your relationship with your former spouse—too busy having fun with your kids, too busy enjoying your life. By reading this book and believing in the need to change your thinking and behavior, you have made the first step toward a new relationship with your ex. Like it was for Jake, it's time to let go of what you cannot control and embrace what you can.

Much like the way Jake first dreamed about getting his neighbor out of his life, you also dream about having your ex out of yours. Friends and acquaintances are often telling you about "a couple they know" who divorced, found other people, and still get together for their kids' birthdays and Christmas. You used to wish you could be one of those divorced couples, but you would now be satisfied with simple peace. Forget friendship, forget joint birthday parties for the kids, and forget opening the presents Christmas morning—just peace. You want peace so much that you can taste it: no more arguing, no more threats, and no more tension. You divorced because of the animosity, but the problem has continued. In fact, it has worsened. It feels like your ex is fueled by thoughts of ruining you. People who get along with their exes—well-meaning people who try to reassure you those things will get better—seem so confident that anybody can do it. When you try to explain your personal situation, how you've tried and tried to make things better, no one truly understands.

That said, people who get along with their exes have a positive attitude and seem happy about the current state of their lives. I believe as humans, we all want to be successful: happy at work, happy in our personal lives, happy as parents, just *happy*. Until you divorced and ended up in this hellish situation, you also thought of yourself as happy. Divorce has shaken everything you thought regarding what it takes to be happy. You've always believed that people who try hard enough ultimately find happiness. This belief was evidenced by the success and happiness you found in your career and as a parent. The difference in your life is the unhappiness, perhaps even outright despair, which you are experiencing in your relationship with your ex. You try to focus on the positive events, positive attributes, and positive experiences, but your ex won't let you be happy. In fact, your ex seems bent on making your life hell.

I'm here to rescue you. You feel lost in the desert with a sandstorm approaching. Not only will I provide you with water and shelter, I'll also provide you with a compass and clear directions on how to find your oasis in the storm. How? Like airtight goggles protect your eyes during a sandstorm, I'm going to shield you from verbal attacks and legal mudslinging with knowledge about why your ex is doing what he is doing; and why he demanded a divorce but won't go away. More importantly, I am going to shield you with internal strength to navigate whatever storm arises. Through self-reflection and personal challenges, you are going to think and behave differently. Then, only after you are fully equipped with your armor of internal and external knowledge, I will help you create an action plan.

What can you expect?

- *to feel happier*
- *to feel like you have options in your life after divorce*
- *to be the best person or parent you can be (even if your ex says otherwise)*
- *to focus on life rather than divorce*
- *to get out of divorce hell*

How can I promise you this when other efforts have failed?

In two words: **empowerment** and **disengagement**. Empowerment has several different interpretations. However, I want you to think of empowerment as the creation of options. When people, men, women, adolescents, and children, believe that they have options, they feel better, are able to be more assertive, and have better self-esteem. Through this book, you will empower yourself with options. When I shield you with knowledge, you will have options to do things differently. You will understand that your ex's behavior has nothing to do with you. His efforts to throw obstacles in the way of your success will not deter you from the life you want to live. You will *feel* empowered to *do* things differently. By following the guide set out in the pages of this book, you will create an action plan for doing things differently. These new behaviors will allow you to completely disengage from the dynamics that harm you. In other words, you will completely disengage from your ex and the behaviors that haunt you. When you do things differently, you will experience empowerment. *Sayonara*, baby! Toodle-oo, Debbie Downer! *Au revoir*, Litigant Larry and your lawyer too!

Embrace the knowledge and follow the strategies, and you will create your own calm. The more consistent you are in applying the strategies you are about to learn, the more success you will feel. The more success you feel, the better the results.

The degree of change you experience will be directly proportionate to the effort you put forth. Remember that, unlike other efforts to improve your relationship with your ex, like separation counseling or mediation, this guide considers that your ex may never make changes. In fact, I err on the side of caution by making the assumption that your ex will *always* try to put you through hell. (He may never feel the need to change. He may never want to do things differently.) While I believe in the power of positive thinking, in cases of high-conflict separation and divorce, I am a realist. I interviewed people who had been in conflict for up to seventeen years—yes, seventeen years! Therefore, my belief in the power of positive lies in my belief that you have the power to think and do better for yourself and your kids. When these changes happen, you will feel positive. I do not want you to wait until your ex is ready to make changes. You owe it to yourself to start now.

Right now, you believe your ex *is* making your life hell. The difference between now and the future is that in the future, your ex can only *try* to make your life hell. *He will not be successful in damaging your self-confidence. He will not be successful in ruining your time with your children.* Your success will not be determined by his behavior—only your own. No matter how hard he *tries* to undermine your success, you will be cognitively and behaviorally equipped to respond appropriately.

Like Jake disengaged from his toxic relationship with his neighbor Norm, you are going to disengage from the miserable relationship you have with your former spouse. This is a process whereby you first take in knowledge, consider how the knowledge affects you and your understanding of your relationship with your ex, and ultimately use this knowledge to frame your thinking and direct your behavior. You will learn to disengage, feel better, and live your life after divorce in a state of calm and contentment!

Who's already disengaged?

As Kimberly, thirty-seven, divorced four years, explained,

I have had people at my house, like friends ... He will come and drop off the kids and he'll come into the entrance and he will leave. These people

will say, "Oh my God! What the hell was his prob-
lem?" and I look up with this stunned look and
say, "What do you mean? He was fine today; that
was nothing." I don't even hear it anymore. He
leaves and I go on with my day.

There's also Angela, forty-one, divorced seven years, who said,

It has come a long way, almost full circle, from
when we could hardly agree on anything with the
children. That was just so frustrating when really
it was like black and white, day and night. We're at
a really good place, everything seems more peace-
ful ... a lot more enjoyment—I don't get worried;
I don't stress. When we get together and meet with
the children, it doesn't bother me at all now.

Finally, there's Mark, thirty-six, divorced three years, who explained,

I am emotionally detached from her now, so I treat it very much like a business relationship. I don't mean it to sound harsh, but we have this job, we have these two amazing kids we have to raise to the best of our abilities. So I have learned, through counseling, how to emotionally disengage so I am not making emotional decisions, and I am not getting sucked into the negative patterns we had for fifteen years.

Give Peace a Chance: A Guide to
Doing Divorce Differently

Regardless of where you live, you can count on some similarities between the designated family law systems. One influential chief justice recently described the family legal system as slow, complex, adversarial, and expensive. As someone who cares about parents and kids, I agree. What this means for the average parent is that when you take your family matter to court, whether to address issues of custody, access, or money, it will cost you. It will cost you time, money, and health. This cost may have already extended beyond the resources available to you. Perhaps you were forced to borrow from family, friends, credit cards, or mortgage your house? If you, or someone you know, have dealt with lawyers, judges, and what many refer to as "divorce war," you know how financially and emotionally costly battling with your ex can be. The 1989 film *The War of the Roses* starring Michael Douglas and Kathleen Turner depicted just how bad divorce can get—people battling to the death over possessions. Perhaps your situation feels equally as terrible. Maybe the court battle has finished but the tension between you and your ex remains.

When a relationship dissolves, typical hurdles to separation involve dividing assets and property (such as selling the matrimonial home) as well as coming to an agreement on child custody and parenting issues. You probably have dealt with the same or similar issues. You may already have spent thousands of dollars attempting to resolve issues with your ex by paying lawyers and bringing issues before judges. You are probably worn out by the loops and hoops brought on by your involvement in the legal system.

I understand that you want things resolved. This desire for resolution is what propels people just like you to spend your life savings to get the toughest lawyer. One lawyer told me that he is often surprised by people's lack of reaction when he tells them that they will be spending a minimum of twenty-five thousand dollars (each!) if the matter goes to trial. While this lawyer used to expect people to react with surprise or even outrage, his reference to such a large financial cost rarely elicits any reaction. "It's like they expect it!" Rational thinking and common sense have been too often disregarded when people approach divorce. Perhaps people entering the divorce process have resigned themselves to handing over savings and hacking into credit to mutually dissolve a relationship. This seems completely irrational. Two consenting adults marry, the same two adults agree to end the marriage but, to make this adult decision, it will cost them thousands upon thousands of dollars? Who benefits from this lack of rational thinking? If you have been privy to experiencing the family law legal system, did you benefit?

Certainly, for the most part, parents do not benefit. They suffer psychological stress and financial devastation. Absolutely, children do not benefit. Just like Nathaniel, they suffer the effects of exposure to conflict between the people they love most: their mom and dad. Children who are exposed to conflict between their parents are at risk of depression, anxiety, and acting-out behaviors. When parents do well after divorce, children do well. This means that if parents don't do well because they are stressed out by the psychological and financial stressors of divorce, their children suffer too.

Who benefits from this lack of rational thinking—this lack of common sense? Common sense would dictate that it is not wise to spend thousands of dollars on legal counsel, documenting negative things about my child's other parent, and ultimately agreeing to pass decision-making to a judge (essentially a man or woman who does not know me, my spouse, or my kids). However, despite common sense and rational thinking, thousands of separating couples do this every day.

So who benefits? Who would you like to see benefit? What would you like to see as the outcome?

At the risk of alienating my legal counterparts, many of whom do their absolute best for their clients, the answer is *lawyers*. Lawyers benefit from the loops and hoops of the family law system. This is not to say that lawyers do not want the best for their clients; most of them do. What this means is that the only people who benefit from your divorce are the people that have the expertise to manage the legalities of dissolving the relationship. If you have not educated yourself about how to best manage your separation and divorce, you are risking your financial and psychological well-being.

This guide is not written for lawyers. It is written for people like you, people who have separated from spouses or partners and want to get on with their lives. That's why this guide has removed the barriers to understanding. There are no loops. There are no hoops. Better yet, there are no unforeseen costs or legal bills!

This guide brings simplicity and commonsense thinking back to the center of solving the problems before you. You and your ex are having problems in your post-separation relationship. You probably had problems prior to your separation as well. Research tells us that problems just don't go away because people separate. In fact, for many divorced people, problems often worsen. Heck, you may have challenges before you that you have not even yet considered!

Common sense. Yes, the kind of sensibility or *thinking* that maybe your grandparents talked about. The kind of thinking that is supposed to send off alarm bells when something just doesn't seem to make sense. Unfortunately, when people are in the process of a divorce, it seems that importance of common sense is minimized—the alarm bells silenced. Instead, people ignore those alarm bells and break every social rule. People approach divorce with strategies they would never even consider in other areas of their lives. Let's take an example: Would you call your boss names if she didn't give you the day off work? Probably not. You may not be happy about having to come into work on a day that you had other important plans, but your common sense would dictate how not to behave in such a circumstance. You would avoid name calling because it would have long-term consequences. So you understand social rules and long-term consequences, but would you call your ex-partner names if she upset you? Hmmm … maybe?

So common sense tells us that saying mean things to your boss doesn't work. Common sense also tells us that writing mean things about your boss to your colleagues also doesn't work. What makes people going through a divorce think that bad behavior or unregulated emotional outbursts will work in their favor when they are dealing with their exes?

I promise you, it doesn't. In fact, on a human level, it only inflames already hurt feelings. It works for lawyers who want to litigate your divorce, but I promise it does not work for you or your kids. This guide works on a human level. This means that I am not concerned with how the courts or lawyers would approach your divorce. Instead, I am concerned with how you are going to live your life as a human—a human with needs and feelings. When we deal with human needs and feelings, divorce becomes a transition in your life rather than a never-ending hell. Except for what you've paid for this book, which equates to about five minutes of your lawyer's hourly tariff, any progress you make is free. You can go ahead and tip yourself.

This book is divided into two sections: 1) Think Twice and 2) Purposeful Action. Each section is of equal importance to your success. I know—you want to know how to fix this situation and fast! You may be tempted to skip the Think Twice section and jump to Purposeful Action. I understand, if you're like me, you often want to skip reading the instructions and just put the thing together; however, I caution you against this.

You will not achieve full empowerment without taking time to embrace the knowledge necessary to think differently. Only with *thinking* comes **empowerment**. I've titled the section Think Twice because I want to ensure that you thoroughly think through the knowledge in this section.

Visualize yourself standing at a busy street corner with four lanes of traffic speeding by. In this situation, given that you must cross this street, should you quickly look both ways and run? What are the risks of such a strategy? Would it be preferable to look both ways *at least twice* before making the dash? What are the benefits of this strategy? You get the point—let's not get run down by a speeding vehicle in an effort to cross the street quickly. Let's think *twice* before we take action. I want you to visualize this busy street **before** you interact with your former partner. There are many things that you can do to make this relationship successful *for you*; the first being to think twice before you take purposeful action.

We've already defined empowerment as being the creation of options. It's hard to take appropriate action if we don't have the knowledge. Without knowledge, we have few options. Without options, we can end up feeling trapped. We all feel vulnerable when we are trapped or cornered, especially when our children are involved. The only way I can empower you to think differently is by giving you knowledge, which is discussed in the first section of this book. Remember: the *why* component is essential to understanding the *how*. You may have asked yourself, *Why is my ex behaving the way he does? Why did my ex want out of the marriage but won't seem to leave me alone?* Perhaps most importantly, *What am I doing to keep him engaged in this way?*

Only after you have obtained the thinking ability—*the knowledge*—to answer your own questions can you determine *how* you are going to change this situation. You will walk away from the Think Twice section feeling enlightened, empowered, and willing to invest in a new plan of action.

If you have participated, willingly or unwillingly, in the family law system, you know that people are expected to get their emotions under control and resolve whatever matter is on the table. If you were unable to manage your emotions, your lawyer likely did most of the talking. In this guide, you speak for yourself. In fact, it is very important that you engage fully in this guide if you are to sustain any of the changes you make. Part of the reason legal agreements fall apart is because people were never really invested in the beginning. They made decisions because they felt like they had no other option, they were out of money, and they were emotionally exhausted. I wish I had a quarter for every time a parent told me,

I spent all my money on my lawyer, and by the time we got before a judge, my lawyer told me I'd better settle because it was the best I was going to get. Why didn't he tell me this before I spent thousands? It was the same offer on the table when we started the process. I settled, but I don't really agree.

As my client Kellie, mother of three boys, explained,

It took six years for my husband to sign off on our divorce agreement. Ten thousand dollars each later, we had the same agreement my first lawyer drafted up.

Unlike in the legal system, in this guide you drive the bus. No passing the keys to a lawyer or a judge who doesn't know you. You are responsible for making your life better, and I am providing you with the tools to achieve this. The first tool is to arm yourself with knowledge.

The second section of the book is entitled Purposeful Action! You probably purchased the book for this section. You want to know how to get out of this hellish situation with your ex. While there is not one simple answer and you will have to develop your own path, the destination is **disengagement**. What does it mean to disengage?

Anna had been separated from her husband Dan for three years. Their custody battle for their three-year-old son Cody had financially devastated both Anna and Dan. Neither the parents nor the child were coping well. Cody seemed unhappy and quiet. Anna was struggling to focus at work and was suffering from physical symptoms associated with depression and exhaustion. Dan had started a new relationship but was struggling to balance Cody's needs and those of his new partner. Anna was furious about Dan's new relationship and blamed Dan for her pain and Cody's difficulties.

On the advice of her family physician, Anna sought counseling. In my sessions with Anna it became clear that Anna believed that the opposite of love is hate. Anna believed that because she no longer loved Dan or was unable to love Dan because he loved someone else, she could only cope with this loss through hate. Therapy supported Anna to understand that the hate she was holding on to was shattering her physically and emotionally. She acknowledged that even in peaceful moments, she comforted herself with feelings of hate. She wrote hateful things about Dan in legal papers, spoke hateful words about Dan to friends and family, and thought hateful thoughts about Dan when she settled into bed at night. When she began to explore the problem from the inside out, she realized that she had allowed hate to become part of her core being. Hate was directing her decision-making and her feelings about life after divorce. Hate was making her sick. Anna did not want to hate, but what could she do? How could she cope without hate? As therapy sessions continued, Anna explored her options. Neither loving Dan in the way that she once did or hating him (as she had done for far too long) were viable options. Fortunately I was able to present Anna with another option, one that she had not yet considered. I suggested to Anna that she could simply disengage. Yes, disengage. Although the love she and Dan felt in their relationship was gone, hate did not need to take over. She could move forward as a parent, an individual, and one day with a new partner, simply by disengaging from the old couple relationship.

While the term **disengage** sounds complex, it simply means to step out of the relationship dynamics that are currently in place. In other words, regardless of how your ex behaves, what he says, or what he does, you will no longer feel the need to participate. This will allow you the freedom to move on with your life. *When people disengage, they take purposeful action to change their thinking and their behavior to separate themselves from a relationship or situation.* As a person seeking to disengage from your ex, you will explore yourself and your behavior, increase your understanding about your relationship with your ex, and ultimately invest in a 28-day action plan to change your thinking and your behavior.

Make a 28-Day Commitment

So you now understand the importance of thinking. You now understand that you will create a customized plan to disengage from your ex. By disengaging from your ex, you will have the opportunity to focus on life after divorce rather than focusing on the divorce itself.

I've asked you to commit to 28 days because you are changing behavior. Behavioral change requires time to implement the behavior and normalize it. This does not mean that after 28 days you are cured! It means that after 28 days, you will have learned to think and behave differently. After 28 days, you will have created an action plan and invested in the strategies necessary to carry the plan out. Beyond the 28-day period, you will need to continue to be conscious of your behaviors—specifically your response to your ex. Remember, we are not expecting your ex's behavior to change. He will continue to be the same difficult ex that he has always been. He will continue to be the thorn in your side that he has always been. After 28 days, it will be you who has changed. It will be you who is willing to do things differently, and, most importantly, it will be you who reaps the benefits.

So because you desire a better life, one free from the negativity of your ex, I want you to thoughtfully consider this contract and agree to the statements, not because a lawyer or judge is telling you to, but because you want to!

Contract with Yourself

Look over this agreement and check off each statement. Check only the statements that you agree to. Revisit this contract when you need fuel to make new decisions for yourself.

Contract for A Better Life After Divorce:

- I will create a new internal compass using the knowledge and strategies provided by Dr. Julie.
- I understand that my new compass will guide my thoughts and behavior in my relationship with my ex.
- I will find the courage to do things differently even when I feel vulnerable.
- I will choose to seek inner peace over emotional release.
- My only response to my ex will be to make things better, not to be right or to seek revenge.
- I will put forth all effort to better this situation, including reading the pages, being thoughtful, and completing the exercises.
- I understand that Dr. Julie is fully committed to helping me reach my goal of having a better life for myself and my children, regardless of how my ex behaves.

Signature:

Date:

You've tried different strategies to make things better with your ex. Why do you keep putting the effort in when it feels like one step forward and two steps back? You will continue to put forth effort because there is a solution. Over the next four weeks, this solution will be evidenced by how you think differently, behave differently, and ultimately feel differently. This is your life after divorce. Now live it.

Section 1

Think Twice

Chapter 1

Every Little Bit Hurts:
Conflict and Kids

Why would you try something new when so many efforts have failed? *Why?* Before you purchased this book, you may have already answered the *why* question. It may seem obvious that how you feel about your ex or how your ex feels about you probably wouldn't matter so much if there wasn't a very special someone counting on you to make it work. That special little someone means everything to you—you go to work every day for her, you make her favorite food, you comfort her when she is ill, you taxi her from activity to activity, never mind hosting those weekend slumber parties! Yet despite all of your sacrifices and investment in making your child's life happy and healthy, you have been unable to fix the thing that matters to her most: your relationship with her other parent. Your child may be well beyond hoping that Mom and Dad will get back together— she just wants you to stop fighting in front of her!

Your child, the person who matters most to you, is part of you both. No matter how much you think you despise your ex, you must determine that you love your child more. That is why

3

you keep working on making the relationship better. That is why you are willing to keep working at it. That is why you are willing to *stop* doing what isn't and hasn't worked for you or your child. *Why?* Bottom line: you and your ex share a child, and there are several years until that child becomes an adult. You *want* to create a parenting relationship with your ex that actually works.

Okay, so that is *why*. Your child matters. Now you want to ask yourself, *what?* What have I done and what am I willing to do to make this work for my child?

As Jill, a twenty-nine-year-old mother of two, explained:

> *I knew that it would be a hard road just because of who he is and his personality. I still have to call him to remind him about the child support payment, as he is always three or four days late. I make the calls about the children rather than my own feelings. It can't be about my feelings. It has to be about the kids and their relationship with him.*

Been There, Done That

You may feel like you've tried everything to make it better. You may have even involved professionals to help make things better. You may have attended separation counseling or agreed to mediation only to end up back in court and still unable to stop the battle. You may even have a final court order after spending tens of thousands of dollars and are still at odds with your ex. It feels like you just can't satisfy your ex, no matter what you do.

Perhaps you have experienced some improvement with these efforts. Your court order confirms that you share decision-making, and you are able to get information that your spouse had previously withheld, like report cards from the school or information from the doctor. Still, the relationship is not where you want it to be. While the face-to-face yelling may have stopped, the undercurrent of tension is still flowing, and you still don't *feel good* about the future of parenting with your ex.

The Power of Knowledge

Take a deep breath. I have good news for all of you emotionally exhausted and financially drained parents. You heard from Angela and Mark in the preface of this book. As these parents and thousands of others across North America have evidenced, it is possible to find happiness in a divorced parenting relationship. Unfortunately, not everyone has been given the tools to do this. If you are in a relationship that is not working, I am here to teach you the strategies that have been left out of traditional approaches, like mediation and separation counseling. These new strategies consider what we know about couple relationships and address the gap left by all of the other efforts you have tried. Are you willing to do something different?

The first strategy that is almost always neglected in mediation and separation approaches is the importance of **arming yourself with knowledge.** Would a firefighter rush into a burning building without first being equipped with adequate training and knowledge of the risks and protective strategies? Definitely not. Perhaps a better question is this: Would the experts responsible for his safety allow this to occur? Probably not. Definitely not if they wanted him to come out alive. The thing is, every day divorced people are left to navigate a highly complex situation with limited to absolutely no knowledge of the factors that create risk or offer protection. Rarely do mediators, lawyers, or judges have or take the time to educate people about what is influencing their situations. In many ways, as professionals working with families during the transition of divorce, we have been negligent in our approaches. We "divorce professionals" have taken a "do as I say" approach with people experiencing divorce. This strategy works with no other clinical population, so why should we believe that it would work with generally competent, intelligent people going through a major life transition? Bottom line: We shouldn't believe it because we have already proven that it doesn't work. The family law divorce system as we know it is broken. People need to know better to do better.

Listen closely: The strategies that you are about to learn go deep into the complex relationship of parenting after divorce. They are embedded in an understanding that the ex-couple relationship is powerful and complex. The ex-couple relationship, like the couple relationship that came before it, is rooted in and influenced by many factors. To successfully parent apart from your ex is complicated. To change the parenting relationship, or to make it livable, you must understand that simply because the couple relationship ends, the dynamics between you and your ex often continue. When counselors and mediators approach parenting after divorce without considering the dynamics established during your couple relationship, the bigger picture is lost and the path to a better life is not clear. In other words, to expect that two people who have not been compatible for years, who have been embroiled in seemingly endless disputes, will suddenly "make things work" in the best interest of their children is completely unrealistic. In fact, as you may have experienced, things can become more difficult after separation and divorce. Your divorce occurred for a reason, and without considering the reason(s) for the demise of the relationship, well-intended efforts may further complicate the parenting relationship with your ex and your ability to be successful in managing it. There are many factors that influence the state of the relationship. Without understanding and considering these factors, turning a *not working* relationship into something better is next to impossible.

You want the parenting relationship with your ex to work. You have experienced what happens when a relationship does not work and countless others can attest to the difficulty of trying to improve the relationship. While I want you to understand that the relationship is complex, I also believe that the strategies to correct the problems need not be. Some of the most complicated problems are solved by the simplest of answers. By following the simple strategies offered through the chapters of this book, you will understand what you need to do to make things better. Not only will you *understand* how to make the relationship better, but you will put together an action plan to create a parenting relationship with your ex that actually works! I am not promising you positive feelings for your ex or that you will ever be friends—this is not the goal. I am offering you an opportunity to parent apart from your ex, live a happy life, and most of all, to completely invest in the emotional needs of your child.

Are you willing?

In my many years of practice with divorced parents, I have treated parents who have been devastated by the conflict in their parenting relationships with their exes. Parents have been financially ruined before deciding to take another path—some had lost post-secondary savings for their children and their own life savings to hold their exes accountable for past wrongs. I have witnessed them do many well-intended things that ultimately made the situation worse. I have also researched what makes parenting relationships after separation and divorce work or not work. I have interviewed parents and allowed them to tell their stories. From these stories, information was analyzed to create a clear picture of what leads to *working* or *not working* parenting relationships after separation and divorce. It is from these experiences that I bring you a strategic plan to make your parenting relationship work.

Throughout the Purposeful Action portion of this book, you will hear the words of real divorced parents; parents who, like you, found themselves in terrible, conflict-ridden relationships with their ex-spouses. Their experiences, combined with clinical knowledge, regular consultation with an experienced family lawyer, and research are intended to help you take a new path toward happiness both as a parent and as an adult with goals and desires that extend beyond divorce. No longer will you need to base every decision upon what you think your ex might do next!

Destination Disengage

Before we talk about how we are going to get there, let's define where we are going. Ultimately, you want to feel better. In the chapters ahead, you will learn how to recover from your divorce migraine. The antidote for a divorce hangover, like pain medication and fluid is to a headache, is achieving **disengagement**. I am not referring solely to disengaging from conflict. We are talking about disengaging from the former couple relationship and dynamics that you shared, and continue to share, with your ex. It is these dynamics that are ruining your ability to successfully parent apart from your ex.

For many parents, the dynamics from their couple relationship carry over into their relationship after separation and divorce.

Many people, including divorce professionals, naively believe that when the couple relationship ceases to exist, so do the dynamics that accompany it. This is false. Dynamics, or the underlying forces in a relationship, influence how people interact, communicate, and make decisions. These dynamics do not simply evaporate because the marriage ends. In fact, problematic dynamics can become more challenging when there is no longer investment in the couple relationship.

Things will be better in your parenting relationship with your ex when these dynamics are addressed. Using the strategies identified ahead, you will learn to step out of these dynamics using your thoughts and your behavior. Through *what you think* and *what you do*, you will begin to manage this relationship differently in order to have a better parenting relationship with your ex.

To achieve dynamic disengagement, you must invest in a strategic plan. In effect you are going to change how you relate to your ex by challenging how you think about him, how you think about yourself and your life after divorce, and how you translate these thoughts into new behaviors. Ultimately you will develop your plan using four key steps:

1. Understand
2. Choose Your Path
3. Regulate to Navigate
4. Self-Attribute

When these strategies are consciously applied to your life and your relationship with your ex, you will be free from your divorce hangover.

You may feel that all too familiar lump in your throat returning or your eyes tearing as you consider the entirety of your situation. You are not alone. Thousands of men and women are going through the emotions that accompany divorce conflict that plays out in parenting and custody matters. I am here to help you build upon your inner strength and successfully parent apart from your ex. You're an ex-spouse, not an ex-parent! Let's get started.

Chapter 2

The Power of Knowledge

A week after my wife told me she wanted a divorce,
she went down to Florida for a vacation and took
all the family money. I looked after the children
for two weeks while she was in Florida. When she
came home, she said, "Thanks for looking after the
children. Now get out of my house, and you'll hear
from my lawyer."—John, divorced four years

I get it—it's hard not knowing what's coming. Perhaps, like John, you were completely taken off guard by your ex's decision to separate. At the time, it felt like you were just going about your daily routine when he told you "it's over." Or, alternatively, maybe you were the one who said "enough" to a marriage that wasn't working, and your ex is angry with you for ending what he thought was for a lifetime. Whatever led up to your separation, the marriage has ended, feelings are hurt, and ultimately you are at odds with your ex. You feel like you are trying awfully hard to be amicable, but it's not working. It's hard to know what to expect. Sometimes you are able to talk, however briefly, but other times you are met with that dreaded piercing glare when you pull into his driveway with the kids. Two weeks ago, he sent you a polite text message asking you to switch weekends with the children, but last week the phone message he left on your voicemail at work made the hairs on your neck stand at attention!

Mixed messages. You've been receiving them since separation. Navigating a parenting relationship after divorce requires you to anticipate receiving mixed messages from your ex. Navigating successfully also requires you to consider that you may also be responsible for sending unintended mixed messages to your ex. This is not because you are a bad person or that your ex suddenly grew horns and began mimicking a demon—for that matter, neither did you. What one, or both of you, is experiencing is lack of **emotional regulation**. You are both experiencing stress and possible anxiety related to your divorce, and you both need to maintain a parenting relationship for your kids. This is hard. Sometimes it feels a bit easier and sometimes it feels harder than it was the day before. This is why you sometimes feel able to deal with your ex and other times the thought of contact with him feels overwhelming. This is why he sometimes seems almost friendly and other times like he will never forgive you.

If you are going to respond effectively to a lack of regulation on the part of your ex-spouse, you must examine and understand your emotions. That's right. By understanding your feelings and emotions, you increase your ability to regulate your behaviors. The benefit of self-regulation (effectively managing your own emotions) is **long-term gain**. This requires you to look beyond what you are feeling to what you want to feel. While an immediate sense of relief may be attained by lashing back at your ex or defending against accusations, there is no long-term benefit to an emotionally-driven response when dealing with an ex-spouse. You need to look beyond what you feel now to what will best allow you to be a happy individual and parent over the long-term. It's self-expression verses self-interest. The latter must be your priority. You may think that you will feel better if you call your ex names, or tell him what a neglectful father he has turned out to be. Maybe for a short time you will. You will blow off all that anger that has been simmering just below your collar bone. I understand that the anger toward your ex sometimes feels like vomit sneaking to the back of your throat. I understand, but I promise that whatever brief relief you feel, you will pay for it over the long term. Think long term. Courts and many mediators will tell you to try to communicate positively or say what you feel politely. I am telling you to *say nothing*. Your ex will be hurt and angered by you sharing your feelings, and you will fuel the fire that you want to put out. Show restraint because it will benefit you. Expressing what you *really* think about your ex *must* matter less, and being a happy parent needs to matter more. Bottom line: It is in your self-interest to regulate your feelings. Remember when you signed the contract on page xxxi agreeing to choose peace over emotional release—this is it!

This chapter arms you with the knowledge necessary to regulate your feelings and manage your behavior with your ex. To help you with this process, I am going to provide you with knowledge keys. Knowledge keys are phrases to support you in looking at your situation differently. They summarize each section of knowledge into a statement. It may be helpful for you to write these knowledge keys on a separate sheet of paper. Otherwise, for convenience, I have provided you with a list at the end of the chapter. You may choose to cut out this list and keep it in your purse or wallet for reference over the next 28 days. For example, here is your first key:

Knowledge Key: Show restraint because

it is in my self-interest to do so.

To regulate those pesky feelings and accomplish the role of a happy, divorced parent, you first need to get out of defense mode. Defense mode is a symptom of the way people typically handle divorce. Defense mode results from the need to show that you are a *better* parent, a *better* person, than your ex. Not only does your ex challenge you in this manner, but the entire legal system puts you in this position. You want to feel better and just get on with your day, but you find yourself defending your history, your decisions, and your role as a parent. In particular, fathers often feel placed in a position where they must justify the importance of their involvement, their *continued* involvement, as a parent after divorce. Mothers, on the other hand, often feel criticized for putting their individual needs above keeping the family together. Both men and women find themselves defending their choices and parenting abilities. This position is fueled by lawyers, affidavits, and an adversarial process that pits one parent against another.

When people are in defense mode, they describe feeling that their exes are out to get them using underhanded tactics such as allegations about poor parenting to outright abuse. Others describe attempts by their exes to take hold of finances or assets, such as homes and other properties. Many reasons lead to people being in defense mode; however, just like it doesn't matter whether it was the wine or the martini that gave you the headache, it doesn't matter what circumstances led to you being stuck in defense mode. You cannot revamp the family court system alone. While the scenarios vary, many parents feel that their only option is to safeguard themselves in a defensive mode. Like Anna felt she was safeguarding herself with hate, other parents feel they protect themselves by staying in defense mode. Both strategies are ineffective. When in defense mode, parents not only spend

14

time responding to actions by their exes, but they also spend time *preparing* to respond to anticipated actions by their exes. If you are not living this yourself, you can only imagine how exhausting and emotionally draining being in defensive mode is! These parents are continually waiting to be attacked; therefore, they become hyper-vigilant to threat. In this state of hyper-vigilance, they are willing to do anything to restore a sense of safety and calm. This makes them vulnerable to emotionally responding to situations rather than rationally thinking twice and then responding.

The consequences of emotional responses to situations of conflict can be dire. For some people, the consequence is exhausted finances through legal battles; for others, it means involving police and child welfare authorities; for most, it means getting very little sleep and not a lot of leisure time due to worrying about what is next. *Next* can mean many things. Remember, you choose your path. To feel better and consequently self-regulate your emotions and behavior, you must get out of your current mode of thinking, feeling, and behaving. To do this, you must take time to understand what is causing this dreadful situation to occur between two people who once cared for one another.

First, if you are responding emotionally, it is because you are taking your ex's behavior personally. Maybe you are also taking his lawyer's behavior personally. Some parents have difficulty understanding why some lawyers seem so aggressive. Lawyers are aggressive on behalf of their clients—not because of you. In fact, your ex's lawyer probably doesn't even know you. I know it feels like it is about you since it is your name that has been dragged through the mud, your name that appears on the court record, and your name that he seems unable to say without loathing. For you and your well-being, however, you cannot take what is being said to you, or about you, personally.

I also know that your experience feels like a unique situation. It is. Your situation is exclusive to you, and I am not minimizing what is happening in your life. However, all divorced parents share some common experiences. For example, for many divorced parents, the stressors after divorce are rooted in issues that occurred prior to separation. Some of these stressors, such as the reason for the separation, affect how well parents get along after divorce. For most people, the process of separation and divorce is an emotionally charged and often conflict-evoking time. When children are involved, sometimes unresolved frustrations between the divorcing spouses are carried out through custody and access disputes. As one mother said to me, "If we didn't have kids, it wouldn't matter. He could be an asshole, and I could still go on with my life." As this mother articulated, unlike divorced people without children, divorced parents are required to maintain contact with their ex, either directly or indirectly. As you've learned through your own experience, it can be very challenging to have a parenting relationship in the absence of the couple relationship. When people experience difficulty in their redefined relationship as divorced *parents*, it is important to accept that challenge is a normal part of separation. To expect otherwise is unreasonable.

Knowledge Key: Don't take it personally.

For divorced parents, the year immediately following divorce has been identified as an important time in which to negotiate and redefine roles within the family system. If you and your ex are still within this time frame, consider that some of these behaviors are symptomatic of the family unit, with Mom, Dad, and kids adjusting to a very different family system than had existed prior to the marital breakup. If you and your ex are well beyond this one-year period since separation, you both may have become more entrenched in how you are interacting. Therefore, to make a shift you must challenge yourself constantly about your thoughts, feelings, and behaviors. This is essential to dynamic disengagement.

It is also important that you understand the context, or circumstances, that surround parenting after divorce. While parenting with an ex is not easy and is ridden with challenges, it can be different—and it can be better. When couples separate, those who report feeling the best are able to understand the emotions behind the behaviors (like sending mixed messages) and are less likely to become stressed and angered by the difficulties in communication. Because they do not take the behaviors of their exes personally, or somehow believe that they can change the behaviors of their exes, they are able to understand and respond rather than react defensively.

I have provided you with the information you need to understand that *this is not personal*. While it feels like a very personal attack on you as a mother, a father, or *a person*, the behavior of your ex is actually his failed attempt to self-regulate his feelings and behavior. The behavior you are seeing is often an effect of an adversarial family law system where divorce pits one member of the family against another. In many ways, you are witnessing your ex emotionally spiral out of control because of the pressure resulting from this process. Don't let him take you down at the same time! To step out of defense mode, increase your ability to regulate emotionally, and not take your ex's behavior personally, you must understand that poor behavior on the part of your ex is simply a product of stress and emotional turmoil—a lack of emotional regulation. You cannot fix this for him or hold him accountable. You may also consider that you and your ex share this common experience of having to cope with feelings and stressors related to the end of a marriage and parenting after divorce.

You and your ex may be sharing other common stressors. You or your ex may also be dealing with stress related to work, finances, or other relationships. Stress is hard on humans, and stress associated with divorce and custody/access battles generally makes people behave poorly.

So you understand that your ex is stressed out and is behaving poorly because of it. Okay. Where does this leave you? After all, you're stressed too, right? When people get caught in this stress-induced emotional havoc, they tend to not look after themselves as well as they should. Simply put, you need to look after yourself. Your ex needs to look after himself too, but you can't control this.

I need you to understand that the mixed messages and inconsistent behavior, whether exhibited by you or your ex, are symptoms of bigger problems: stress and emotional turmoil after divorce. When you don't deal with stress, you are vulnerable to being hurt and frustrated by those you perceive to be responsible for all the wrongs in your life. While your ex may be the stressor receiving the most attention in your life, life stress is rarely rooted in one source. While possibly deserving of the primary blame, your ex does not control how you feel about yourself or your life. Remember Jake? Clearly Norm the neighbor played a role in creating unhappiness for Jake, but ultimately it was up to Jake to make his life happy again. In other words, we are responsible for what we do and how we live regardless of what provokes us.

Stress provokes bad behavior from both you and your ex. Stress also provokes inconsistent behavior, where one day communication feels okay and the next day it feels impossible. People who do better after divorce make a plan to have less stress during their free time and less stress at work, and they understand the importance of friends and family in helping them through difficult times.

Your Internal Dialogue

To shift out of defense mode, you need to incorporate what you understand from the above paragraphs with what you are thinking and saying to yourself – therapists refer to this as your *internal dialogue*. What thoughts come to mind when I ask the question, "Tell me about parenting after divorce?"

Jim, a forty-five-year-old airline pilot stated,

> *It's hell—my ex is out to get me. She doesn't want me to have time with the kids, and she's got a law-yer from hell that hates men and wants every cent I've worked for.*

So that's how Jim thinks he feels about parenting after divorce. We can tell that he is angry about his relationship with his ex-wife. We can tell that he is frustrated by the financial fallout from the divorce. We can tell that he doesn't like his ex-wife's lawyer. Jim has quite a divorce migraine. It sounds like he feels miserable and is suffering. Despite my initial question, his response does not tell us how he feels about being a parent after divorce.

Because Jim is caught up in the emotional turmoil of divorce, what he missed was a key word in the question: *parenting*. Did you notice that in all of Jim's response, his only mention of his children was in relation to his ex-wife? Jim stated, "It's hell—**my ex** is out to get me. **She** doesn't want me to have time with the kids, and **she**'s got a lawyer from hell who hates men and wants every cent I've worked for." Jim, like so many parents embroiled in conflict with their ex-spouses, is caught up in identifying primarily as an ex-spouse rather than as a parent. His focus to a question about parenting demonstrates that his view about life after divorce centers on being an ex-husband, not a parent.

I understand that Jim feels hurt and betrayed by his ex-wife. Jim does not need to pretend that he has a positive relationship with his ex-wife, but he would benefit from redirecting his thoughts toward being a parent rather than being an ex. By doing so, he would purposely focus on how he enjoys his children instead of how much he does not like his ex-wife. By changing the focus, he fuels positive emotions (like his love for his children) rather than reinforcing the anger and frustration that is distressing him. A simple change in the response could acknowledge problems in his relationship with his ex, yet focus his primary energy on being a dad. It might sound like this, "Well, my ex and I have problems, but as a father, I love my children and want to spend time doing things we enjoy, like playing outdoors and going to the beach." In this response, Jim has offset his anger and frustration with fueling thoughts about his role as a dad to children that he loves being with. The focus is on *I*, which demonstrates a sense of responsibility for self, rather than on *her*, which demonstrates a sense of victimization. The focus is also on Jim's role as a parent with an understanding that this *parent* identity dominates his *ex-spouse* identity.

Let me ask you the same question I asked Jim. Tell me about parenting after divorce. First, I want you to answer with the first thoughts that enter your mind:

_____

_____

_____

_____

_____

Okay. Now read your response out loud. Like I highlighted key words in Jim's response, I would like you to do the same. Did you use words primarily about your ex, or did you talk about being a mom or dad? Do your words reflect anger and frustration, or do they talk about enjoyment, love, or things that make you happy? Do you use *I, he, or him?* Every word matters.

I am now asking you the same question again. Tell me about parenting after divorce. This time I want you to pause, think twice, and formulate your answer in a way that focuses not on your feelings about being an *ex*-husband or *ex*-wife, but that centers on you as a mom or dad to your children who you love very much. So tell me about parenting after divorce:

_____

_____

_____

_____

_____

What we say internally (to ourselves) will reflect what we think. In turn, what we think reflects how we feel. I need you to understand that the process of changing how we feel requires us to change what we think and what we do. If you want to be a happier parent after divorce, you need to change your internal dialogue. If you make statements like, "My ex is out to get me; my ex is ruining my life," your life will feel ruined. However, if you make statements like, "I am a good parent; my children love me," you are telling yourself that you have a good life *despite* your ex. You are also differentiating between your role as an ex-spouse and your role as a parent. Stop spending so much time thinking about how being your ex is hurting you and start thinking about how much being a parent is giving you!

Knowledge Key: My happiness is not part of the divorce settlement.

What do you love about being a parent *despite* having problems with your ex?

When you realize that you have been giving your power to be happy away to the person you trust least, you will be able to embrace your role as a parent after divorce. You will begin to spend less time thinking about your ex, and you will stop formulating how you are going to defend yourself from whatever he throws at you. Slowly, you will begin to change how you think about your ex. The behavior that you are seeing from your ex, such as being nice one day and not the next, is not your problem. That is his problem. The texts, e-mails, and posts on Twitter belong to him, not you. What your ex says to you is not your problem. You will no longer need to defend yourself against things that have nothing to do with you. The mixed messages and hurtful behavior are symptoms of your ex's inability to manage stress effectively. The mixed messages you are receiving from your ex are likely the result of the stressors in his life (yes, you may be one of them) as opposed to things that you are doing. You cannot change his behavior, only your own.

Now, if you are engaging in the mudslinging and mixed messages, you are also failing to manage your stress associated with divorce effectively. Long-term gain comes with focus on self-care, reducing stress, and investing in life after divorce, not the divorce itself. It comes with a willingness to embrace responsibility for your happiness, for your child's happiness, and your future.

When you understand your feelings and behavior as well as that of your ex in a different way, you learn that you do not need to defend yourself. In fact, by stepping back and not becoming defensive, you clearly send the message that the attack does not require a response. You send the message that the behavior of your ex, his feelings, his words, and the words of his lawyer will not influence how you choose to live your life as a parent after divorce. Your focus shifts to being a parent after divorce, not being an ex-spouse. You are out of defense mode and into living as a parent after divorce.

Knowledge Keys:

Show restraint because it is in my self-interest to do so.
Don't take it personally.
My happiness is not part of the divorce settlement.

Section 2

Purposeful Action!

Chapter 3

From This Moment On: Dynamic Disengagement

I am emotionally detached from her now, so I treat parenting with her much like a business relationship. I don't mean it to sound harsh, but we have this job. We have these two amazing kids that we have to raise to the best of our ability. I have learned how to emotionally disengage so I am not making emotional decisions, and I am no longer getting sucked into the negative patterns we had for fifteen years.—Matthew, divorced three years

Understanding Dynamic Disengagement

The action of dynamic disengagement involves purposefully removing yourself from the interactions that are problematic in your parenting relationship with your ex. While simple in definition, given the emotionally charged, often disempowering situation of parenting with someone you do not get along with, this can be challenging.

Overall, the path to dynamic disengagement requires you to rework what you are currently doing. In some cases, this means you must throw out your current strategies and completely rebuild your tool kit for approaching this new phase in your life. Parenting after divorce does not come with a step-by-step guide; however, as you disengage, you will create your customized plan that works *for you*.

Starting from the Inside

Everything that clinicians and researchers know about happiness suggests that true happiness, the kind that brings with it feelings of peace and contentment, must come from within. In other words, how we feel about ourselves and our ability to navigate our world affects how we feel. Therapists refer to this as having healthy self-esteem and self-confidence. Some people spend much of their adult lives building self-esteem while others have never thought it to be lacking. When people have healthy self-esteem and self-confidence, they feel capable of responding to and improving life circumstances.

Unfortunately, life events such as divorce can challenge our self-esteem and shake our self-confidence. That's why you need to take a snapshot of how you are feeling at this time. A lot may have changed since your relationship ended. Perhaps some things stayed the same. This is an exercise to look at you—not your relationship with your ex, but you as a divorced, individual person with children. Look around you. Where are you living? Who are the people in your life? Who are your friends? Where do you work? What is your financial situation? Who do you turn to when you need someone to talk to?

To make things easier, complete the following My Profile exercise. This exercise will help you identify the strengths and obstacles in your life. Simply circle your response to each question.

My Profile

1. Problems with my ex are hurting me.   YES   NO
2. I believe things can be better.   YES   NO
3. I have people in my life who care about me.   YES   NO
4. I am happy in my relationship with my child.   YES   NO
5. I am happy with how I look physically.   YES   NO
6. I have good physical health.   YES   NO
7. I am a good person.   YES   NO
8. Other people like me.   YES   NO
9. I have a supportive family.   YES   NO
10. I am happy with my financial situation.   YES   NO
11. I am part of a larger community.   YES   NO
12. I have friends who care about me.   YES   NO
13. I enjoy my work.   YES   NO
14. I used to like my ex.   YES   NO
15. I have many strengths.   YES   NO
16. I am a spiritual person.   YES   NO
17. I am able to reach goals.   YES   NO
18. I get along with people at work.   YES   NO
19. People respect me.   YES   NO
20. I respect myself.   YES   NO

Preparing to Begin the Path toward

Dynamic Disengagement

You've taken a snapshot of your life before disengagement. Now it is time to begin to disengage. To initiate your individualized journey, it is necessary to consider what would make parenting with your ex better. This is different for everyone. Your mind may feel blank as you explore this question! *What would make parenting with my ex better?* Perhaps you are so caught up in putting out fires or ensuring that you dodge the legal mudslinging that you haven't stopped to think about how you will know when the relationship is better. Perhaps you would know that things are better when you are able to drop your son off at his home rather than meeting at a public place? Maybe you could go to your daughter's soccer game without worrying that your ex might sit in the same section as you?

I understand that these questions may seem too big to answer quickly. However, if you don't know where you are going, it is hard to draw a map of how to get there. Think about where you are in your relationship with your ex at this time. Are you able to speak in person? Over the phone? By text? Not at all? How do you cope with being in the same place at the same time? Finally, how would you know that the relationship had improved?

Take a moment and jot down your initial thoughts about what would look different if your relationship with your ex was better. As Darren, father of Lucas, age seven, reported, "I would know things were better if we could both sit in the same section at the soccer game without me feeling sick to my stomach."

Similarly, Andrea, mother of Aiden, age thirteen, and Reese, age eleven, described that she would know things were better if she behaved differently in situations that currently cause stress. She stated, "I would know things were better if I could call on him to take one of the kids to an appointment when I can't get away from work. Right now, I would never do that because he would hold it over my head forever."

What would be different for you?

If my relationship with my ex was better I would be able to:

_____

_____

_____

_____

_____

_____

_____

The Clean Up: Ridding the Path of Obstacles

To get better, you must ensure that your environment supports healing. If you suffer from medical migraines, you may avoid florescent lights. If you're a recovering alcoholic, you probably don't spend your Friday nights at a bar. Similarly, when you want to recover from a divorce migraine, you cannot surround yourself with the things that remind you of all that is wrong with your ex, all the money he has cost you, and all the grief he has created. When you accept this need for physical change, you are ready to prepare for the process of disengagement.

Together we are ready to *clear the path.* Look around your environment: your home, your apartment, your office, your car. You need to rid your physical space of those things that are obstacles to thinking differently. As a starting point, if you have a collection of legal documents, nasty letters, and affidavits, or your calendar notes everything your spouse has failed to do or has done wrong, you need to *get rid of that collection!* If you have been using e-mail as a way of documenting problems in communication or failures on the part of your spouse to communicate in a meaningful way, *get rid of the documentation!* If you have been saving nasty text messages or voice mails from your ex, *get rid of them!* It is like going on a new eating plan and ridding your home of junk food. *These things are poisonous to your success!* Would you fill your pantry with chips and cookies the day before you start your nutritional plan? Certainly not if you want to achieve success. The same applies to creating a plan for success in your parenting relationship with your ex.

You have control over your environment. You have the power to create an environment where good things can happen. The couple relationship is over, and your room is filled with reminders of everything that continues to be wrong! *Get rid of the reminders!* Shred, burn, recycle—it doesn't matter the mode of purging; what matters is that you are freeing yourself and allowing a new process to take place. Consider the paper, messages, texts, and legal reminders to be a sea of negativity that will drown you if you don't get out from underneath it. The only way to save yourself from the negativity is to get rid of it. Experience tells us that these things will not be important in your new life—your livable, divorced, migraine-free life, that is.

I understand that you have been documenting for a reason. You want to make sure you have your paper ammunition ready when your ex fires the next accusation or complaint. The problem is, your ex may never move forward. The mudslinging from the other side may continue until your kids leave for college. Perhaps your ex likes making you miserable, or maybe he simply does not know how to change things for the better. Regardless of what fuels his behavior, it is up to him to figure it out. You have to understand that by waiting and preparing for his next attack, you are allowing yourself to follow his timeline for when you can move forward. You are saying, "Okay Ex, you tell me when I can be happy again and live my life. You tell me when we can just be parents instead of people at war." Does this sound reasonable? Do you want your ex to tell you how to live, how to parent, whether you can be happy? Probably not.

As you visualize how things can be better, first you must emphasize *self* over *other*. That is, your energy must go into changing your behavior, not that of your ex. Although you might like it to be otherwise, you cannot control your ex. Fortunately, you can control how you respond to his behavior. When you separated, you made a conscious decision to end your couple relationship. You are no longer moving forward as a couple; you are an individual who must have a relationship with another individual because you share a child. Because you made a decision to have a child with this person, there is an obligation to treat this person with respect—not because you like him, not because he gives you respect in return, but because it is your job as a parent. If you truly want to make things better, to live your life without the burden of conflict and negativity, you must decide that you will no longer accept a situation of conflict for you or your child. In effect, you are leaving the firing range. Your ex can decide to remain on the range, but you are making the choice that this is not where you want to spend your life after divorce.

What do you want? Do you want to be at the park with your kids, watching them play ball, driving them to soccer practice, focusing on their homework? Do you want to continue to document everything that continues to be wrong with your ex? Because you are separated and the couple relationship is over, you don't have to wait for your ex to make a good decision. You can create a livable, happy, post-divorce existence whether your ex likes it or not. You are no longer together; you are parenting apart. You are an individual. You have decided to make an essential behavioral change that will make your life, and that of your child, better. You have the power to decide to *do* things differently.

Before you can do things differently, there is something else in your way. You spent years as a husband, as a wife, as a partner. You may have committed fully to this relationship—invested all you had in what you planned it would be. You may have been devastated by the break-up. You believe that you have accepted that this relationship is over, with no more attempts at reconciliation. You are parents in the absence of being a couple. For some, the transition to parenting apart is painful, and for all who make this shift, it is not without challenges. To move forward and successfully parent apart with someone you once loved and who once loved you, you must find acceptance in the changes that have occurred. Roles have shifted, homes have changed, finances have been depleted, and the family makeup is altered. Yet, however emotionally and financially draining this transition has been, you are here. Your kids are here. You are ready to move forward from your couple relationship. Perhaps you felt you were ready to move forward long ago, but your former spouse has impeded this process. You can wait no longer for him to give you the go-ahead. Letting go of the couple relationship allows you a clear path toward dynamic disengagement. Let's go, with or without your ex.

You're Ready to Let Go

Find a quiet place to work through the following paragraphs. A quiet place may be difficult to find when you are parenting on your own, but everyone, especially your child, will benefit by these efforts. Once you are settled into a comfortable, relaxed setting, I want you to ask yourself, *What is my life like now?*

You may feel trapped. The constant conflict and negative interaction with your ex is overwhelming. You thought that the separation would allow you both to move on with your lives. Yes, you knew that it wouldn't be easy; there would still be things you would find difficult, but this? In your wildest dreams, you could not have imagined the problems you have encountered since parting ways with your spouse. Parenting after divorce seems more difficult than when you were together.

At one time, however long ago, you may have considered your ex to be your closest friend—someone you turned to during periods of stress or difficulty. You decided to have a child or children with this person. You may have completely invested yourself in your marriage, and the loss of your best friend has been more difficult than the loss of your intimate partner. For whatever reason during the course of your relationship, things changed, the relationship became difficult, and you separated. By the time you purchased this book, it was a relationship laden with conflict. While the parenting part of the relationship continued, the friendship and intimacy of your couple relationship is gone. Perhaps you feel that you did your best to hold onto the positive aspects of your relationship, but you feel that your ex only wants to argue with you. Maybe you feel like he is trying to cut you out of your child's life. Maybe you feel that he is still trying to control you. Perhaps you felt saddened by the loss of your marriage and in understanding why the relationship became so dysfunctional. The intimacy of your relationship may have faded, or perhaps something or someone created a situation that resulted in broken trust. This has made negotiation difficult, perhaps even impossible.

Yes, you've tried mediation. Problem is, what you agreed upon has changed, and what you thought was resolved keeps resurfacing as a problem. The bills from your lawyer keep coming. Heck, you could have put your first child through college with the amount you've spent fighting to spend time with your kids.

Dr. Julie Gowthorpe, R.S.W.

Your once highly supportive workplace has grown tired of the time off work you require for appointments and court dates.

To develop a parenting relationship with your ex that works, you must start to think about yourself and your life differently. In many ways, a bad relationship with an ex can be like coping with chronic pain. Chronic pain differs from most pain because it extends well beyond the period of normal healing. Given that you are reading this book, I assume that your relationship with your ex has not healed since separation. In cases of chronic pain, treatment assists the patient in moving from *being sick* to *being healthy* in spite of the pain. Through psychological treatment, the patient learns to accept the pain as part of her life. The patient identifies what allows her to best manage the pain, and then she sets expectations that are attainable. Ultimately, the patient develops the ability to cognitively process the pain in a less detrimental manner, whereby the patient perceives the pain as manageable rather than something that is preventing her from living.

Although a relationship with an ex-spouse is different from a condition like chronic pain, for many, the negative situation with one's ex is a *chronic* situation whereby problems in the relationship do not improve in a reasonable time. When people with chronic pain learn to think about and process their pain experience differently, their quality of life improves. Similarly, when people in conflict with their exes learn to think about and process their experiences differently, their quality of life also improves.

This brings us to *how:* How do you process this relationship differently? I have already asked you to consider what your life is like now. I now want you to consider what your life as a parent after divorce could be. Better yet, what would you like it to be? As you begin to contemplate this question, I want you to insert a second, or sub-question: *If my relationship with my ex was helpful rather than harmful, how would my life as a divorced parent be different?*

36

(Take your time, and repeat this question to yourself as many times as you need.)

_____

_____

_____

_____

_____

_____

_____

Here we begin the process of parenting apart in a way that works for you. For clarity, let's come back to the chronic pain parallel. When people suffering from chronic pain get better, it is not because the level of pain has actually changed. They begin to understand that although the chronic pain will not go away or change, they are responsible for the course of their lives and the feelings that accompany their day-to-day decision-making. Some would suggest that they learn to manage chronic pain by considering the positive changes that have resulted from their circumstances. You will need to do the same thing.

Some people feel unable to look at their chronic pain as something other than debilitating. For these people, chronic pain is nothing more than something that makes them disabled and sick. This is their experience. They experience depression and anxiety from their condition. Similarly, when parents become locked in conflict, the last thing they can think of is how their relationship with their adversary can be beneficial! You feel like your ex is making you sick! Research that explores conflict after divorce repeatedly shows that men and women in these situations are more likely to feel depressed and anxious than those who have more positive relationships with their exes.

Like people suffering from chronic pain who decide to live well in spite of their physical condition, you must decide to be the person who, *despite* your relationship with your ex, lives happily and parents happily. You have already initiated the process to visualize "the better." Simply by sitting in a quiet spot, you have given your mind the opportunity for openness, the opportunity to see things differently. Before we get to your ex, we need to talk about you.

Remember that you are a participant in this interaction between two people—only you can allow the pattern to continue or cease. This is not to say that you are entirely responsible for the problem. Sometimes it only takes one person to completely upset a parenting relationship after divorce. That said, even if your ex is creating the problem, you have control over your life and can be happy in spite of this. It really is *all about you*. You will think differently. You will make different behavioral choices. You will make your situation better. You will make your life happier.

To clear your path, I am asking you to avoid visualizing you and your ex working things out together. You are no longer a couple, and you have proven that you cannot work together successfully. I want you to visualize yourself as an individual being happy. To date, you have been disappointed by this failure to have a happy, communicative parenting relationship with your ex. This is why I am not asking you to negotiate with your ex. That road has already been walked with little success. Instead, I am asking you to step outside of the box you may have encountered through mediation or separation counseling, where you were asked to find a middle ground between two polar opposites. I am not asking you to negotiate with your ex; I am asking you to understand that the dynamics of your ex-couple relationship may be undermining your parenting relationship.

Where are you at now? How would you describe parenting with your ex? One father, divorced three years, described his relationship with his ex-wife by saying, "Right now I don't have a lot of love for her. I think that she has turned vicious and vindictive ... I don't know what her goal is because of this pending case conference. I don't know if she is trying to discredit my abilities as a parent or what, but I think that is where she is. I don't think it's healthy; I don't think it's healthy for me. I don't think it's good for her, but it's her business."

Take a moment. How would you describe your parenting relationship with your ex? Some people are able to sum up their relationship in a few words while others take pages. Do what feels comfortable for you. Remember, this is your first step toward disengagement.

I describe my relationship with my ex to others by saying,

_____

_____

_____

_____

_____

Great! You have made the first step in creating a parenting-apart strategic plan—your path to dynamic disengagement. You have taken a look at the world around you and, perhaps equally as important, thought about how you want your world to be. You are visualizing "the better." The chapters ahead will be filled with many exercises to help you move to the place you want to be.

Before you move to the next chapter, turn back to the My Profile on page 29. On the lines below, rewrite only the statements that you answered yes to. For example, if you answered yes to "I have friends who care about me," rewrite that statement on a line below. If you answered no to that same statement, do not rewrite it. We are building upon strengths as we move toward "the better." Don't worry about how many yes and how many no statements you have on your list. At this moment, it's the yes statements that count!

_____

_____

_____

_____

_____

_____

Making a parenting relationship with an ex-partner work is not easy. For example, in Sarah's case, she was furious for her ex-husband for having an affair with a woman from his office. However, despite her anger, she did not want a divorce, even after he admitted that he wanted his relationship with the other woman to continue. Her feelings about the divorce and the lack of control she experienced when her husband ended the marriage complicated the parenting relationship, but they did not prevent it from working. You may be in a similar situation whereby your feelings about your ex and the relationship you shared are creating complications in your parenting relationship. That's okay. You will learn to accept the complexity of this new relationship and work with it rather than against it.

Before you complete this chapter, please take a moment and read to yourself the statements that you have just written from My

Profile. Now, I want you to close your eyes (after you've finished reading this sentence) and consider these words to be the fuel that you need to move forward. When you are thirsty, these words offer you hydration. When you are out of gas, these words will start your engine.

Now think about this word: *resilient*. When someone is resilient, it means that when she experiences a trauma, crisis, or negative life event, she comes through the difficult situation maintaining the same or better psychological state than prior to the experience. For example, some children are incredibly resilient whereby they survive major traumatic events, such as natural disasters or abuse, and yet develop into functioning, successful adults. In other words, they bounce back! We know from research that those things identified in the My Profile exercise have the power to support resilience. The things you have answered yes to will help you heal and recover from this challenging time in your life so that you can be the best person you have ever been. Don't worry if your list is short at this time; when you realize how powerful you are to change this situation, the yes list will grow, and you will reach beyond what you ever thought was possible in your life after divorce.

You are ready to proceed to the next chapter. Don't lose sight of how much better life can be. Enjoy your journey and savor the moments with your precious children.

Chapter 4

Own Your Own Way

You and you alone have the power to make parenting apart better. Unhappy divorced people tend to blame others for making their lives less successful than they believe they should be. They view their lives after divorce with the presumption, "If only this hadn't happened to me, my life would be better." In contrast, happier divorced people accept that they are responsible for the direction of their lives after divorce. They do not attribute this responsibility to their exes, to their lawyers, or to other people in their lives. Happier divorced people are often able to reflect on positive times during their relationships with their exes while also recognizing that the relationship is over. They accept the reality of the situation and do not romanticize what could have been. With this reality, they arm themselves with positive thoughts, a refusal to fuel conflict, and a willingness to separate their feelings from their behaviors.

While it sometimes feels better to have someone else "hold the bag" for problems, we all know that the risk of passing responsibility to someone else is that we have no control over the outcome. By welcoming responsibility, no matter how challenging, we also allow ourselves to assume control over our destinies. Besides, if we leave our happiness to our exes, we could be waiting a long time for things to get better. Waiting for others to change before we make effort to change is not a good strategy. It's not a good strategy in intact marriages, and it is truly a terrible strategy for divorced parents. "I'll do better when you do better" leaves people stuck in limbo. Would you wait for your coworker to get a raise before you do? You purchased this book because you want to get "unstuck." You want your life to be happier whether your ex wants to be happier or not. I am not naive enough to think that your ex will suddenly change his behavior to be helpful to you. *I believe that you can change your thoughts and behavior to be happier without your ex doing anything differently.*

To clear the path to a new and better parenting relationship, you must accept that the onus is on you to make things better. You are the only person in this relationship that you can control. Research shows that people who assume personal responsibility for themselves and their feelings after divorce are far happier than those who attribute their feelings or unhappiness to their exes, regardless of their exes' behavior. So you must learn to think about you and your relationship with your ex differently.

Self-Identity: The Importance of You

There is strong evidence that communication and problem-solving are important predictors for success after divorce. This makes sense because when people are able to talk about issues and then problem-solve scenarios, they are going to be more satisfied with their relationships with their exes after divorce. While communication and problem-solving is beneficial if both parents are participating, there is also evidence that how you cope individually (meaning *in spite of* your ex) yields similar results. In other words, you do not need your ex to communicate with you or problem-solve issues successfully in order for you to be happy parenting after divorce. While parenting after divorce requires you and your ex to share responsibility at least on some level, you may never achieve open communication. Why is this?

Some people learn to communicate and get along with their exes while others do not. One reason that people struggle with communication after divorce is because they have difficulty defining their roles when the couple relationship ends. New, non-couple, parenting relationships pose difficulty for some parents. Like Joe, many people have difficulty seeing themselves as a parent without also identifying themselves as an ex-husband, ex-wife, or ex-partner. When the role of the ex-spouse dominates how you identify yourself or how you respond to questions about life after divorce, people can become stuck in the anger and emotional turmoil of what can be a never-ending process of grieving a lost marriage. Some research has suggested that, following separation, men have greater difficulty with redefining their role from being a husband and father to that of being solely a father. To make the role of being a parent predominant in how divorced people self-identify, divorced parents must let go of their roles of a spouse while holding onto their roles as a parent with an ex-spouse still in the picture. In other words, divorced people with children must accept that while they are parenting the same child or children, they will do this in the absence of the affection once shared in their couple or marital relationship. Their former partners are no longer obligated to care for them as a loving spouse, only to interact with them as another parent. With this loss of partner affection, some parents struggle with the absence of emotional closeness once shared in the parental relationship. They must learn to parent apart from someone with whom they once shared intimacy and love. In an effort to create emotional closeness, some ex partners create issues, however destructive, to necessitate a response from their former spouses. Consider your interactions with your ex since you separated. How did you make this transition from parenting with a spouse to parenting apart without the couple relationship? Do you feel like you've successfully made this adjustment?

When we understand our emotions, we are better able to understand the behavior of others. Before reading this chapter, you may have felt that your ex's behavior was unpredictable, like you never knew what to expect from him, like his anger came out of nowhere. Perhaps your ex is stuck in the marriage, the couple relationship, or the divorce itself—it doesn't matter. Like you, his behavior is symptomatic of his feelings and how he views himself.

Separation and divorce are emotionally charged, often conflict-evoking times for many parents, and the separation process, particularly when adversarial in nature, may have implications for how divorced people view themselves and their places in this world. When children are involved, this separation process can be highly stressful, as divorced parents are required to maintain contact with their former spouses, either directly or indirectly. This required contact with the former spouse triggers feelings about the couple relationship, the loss of the couple relationship, and the vulnerability experienced through the separation process.

As Kim, a thirty-six-year-old mother of preteen girls described:

I tell people that I'm a mom. I also work in mar-

keting so I tell them that too. That is what I always

say first, but then they look at me like they want

to know more. So I tell them about how I got here

and that's when all the feelings come in ... the an-

ger, the hurt. I once loved him, but now I hate him

and it's been years (since the divorce).

From Kim's words, it is clear that when she focuses on her life as an individual, a mother, and a marketer, she feels positive. Unfortunately, as soon as she revisits the divorce and the loss of the loving relationship, negative feelings are triggered and the positive gains minimized. Kim, like you, benefits by focusing on the present—her identify as a mother, professional, and an individual.

How do you identify yourself? Are you a parent? Are you an ex-spouse? If both, where do you focus your energy?

I would describe myself as:

_____

_____

_____

_____

_____

_____

I have asked you to think about you and how you view yourself as a divorced parent. Through this chapter, you have challenged your feelings and how you are going to process situations that arise in your parenting relationship with your ex. You have taken the time to understand your emotions, and you've decided that you don't need to wait any longer for your ex to figure out what he is feeling. Because you have taken this time, your behavior will no longer be guided by the behavior of your ex. You are responsible for your happiness, and it feels great!

As you worked your way through this chapter, I have challenged you to think about how you view yourself as a parent after divorce. I have also challenged you to accept responsibility (it's a good thing!) for your path as a parent after divorce. It can be one of happiness, or it can continue to be what you have been coping with. For divorced parents, the year immediately following divorce has been identified as an important time in which to negotiate and redefine roles as they learn to interact differently with someone they once loved. Men and women experience this rebuilding process differently, but both benefit from the support of family, friends, and self-care strategies as they begin the chapter of happiness after divorce. Remember that you are resilient! You will grow through this experience, and you will create a better, happier life for you and your children.

Chapter 5

The Power of Silence

I would rather run into a burning building than have to listen to her rant one more time about how she feels.—Matt, divorced one year

Self-interest verses self-expression. Ideally, we develop the ability to ensure our self-interests are met by the way we express ourselves as we grow from childhood to adolescence to adulthood. Some of us do this better than others. We all know people in our lives that are exceptionally good at getting what they want through self-expression. We may refer to them as *good communicators*, or *persuasive negotiators*. Because of this ability, you may see them influence decision-making or negotiate change in their own self-interest.

In contrast, we all know other people who display unbridled self-expression regardless of the situation. Think about a friend, a coworker, or an acquaintance that is committed to saying how she feels regardless of how others receive it. While her uninhibited honesty may be appreciated from time to time, chances are she has hurt feelings, evoked anger, and eventually lost relationships due her unwillingness to filter her expression. At times, it was not in her *self-interest* to express her feelings.

During the separation process and as you develop a parenting relationship after divorce, you must accept that it is not in your self-interest to express your negative feelings to your ex. To have a successful relationship with your ex, you must invest in filtering your self-expression. Take the example provided by Matt at the beginning of this chapter. From his perspective, his former spouse "rants" about her feelings. This behavior did not result in his empathizing with her; instead, he was frustrated by this behavior and would do anything to avoid having to listen to her. This type of exchange is not helpful for either party. Having met with Matt, I know that he struggled with not responding to his former wife. If he were to express his feelings, call her names, and suggest that she was "crazy," an already negative situation would have deteriorated further. Instead, choosing self-interest over self-expression, Matt used other resources available to him—family, friends, and his therapist—to express his feelings. This allowed him to avoid a cycle of self-expression that fails divorced parents and their children. Matt was able to move forward and focus on his children and his happiness. He explained:

I can't say things to her anymore because it causes more problems than anything. Sometimes I just needed to vent but it just made things worse. I decided to see a counselor, which got me to open up and deal with different things. That's where I got my support from.

Separated or divorced men and women who vent to their ex-spouses are choosing self-expression over self-interest. Those who remain silent in the face of frustration are thinking "Short term pain for long term gain!" Some of us are better at this than others. Some children understand that they get what they want by adhering to social rules and expectations. Others, unable to self-regulate, express their feelings in an uncontrolled manner, behaviorally acting out or defiantly challenging basic rules. As young adults, we learn to balance self-expression and self-interest. We decide what we are willing to risk in the name of self-expression. The balance between self-expression and self-interest is challenged throughout our life experiences—at work, in friendships, and in marriages. It is never more challenged than when we enter the divorce process.

The good news is that this challenge is manageable. Do you remember the child in your grade school class who just couldn't seem to remember to raise his hand before asking a question, or the girl who never understood that lining up is a strategy to get what you need, say, water from the fountain? The point is, some of us are able to follow a process to get what we want or what we need. Some of us struggle with process and do not like following steps. When working with children, the most successful teachers are able to find simple or achievable steps to solve what seem like complex problems. The best teachers are also able to show the benefit of process—like standing in line for the fountain so no one gets their teeth knocked out on the faucet—to the most challenging of students.

By purchasing this book, you have asked me to break down a very complex problem— navigating the divorced parent relationship—into simple, achievable steps. Like the firefighter who taught you to stop, drop, and roll, I want you to **Understand;**

Choose Your Path; Regulate to Navigate; and Self-Attribute.

In previous chapters, I provided you with the information necessary to put your relationship into context. That is, I gave you the information you need to understand what you are going through so that you could clear your path to dynamic disengagement. I also gave you exercises to examine what you believe about yourself in order to regulate your emotions and behavior. I asked you to consider what your ex is going through, not because I want you to empathize or feel badly, but to equip you with the understanding necessary to make this situation better.

Now, like you learned to stop before you drop and roll, I am asking you to stop before you respond. When you stop, you need to listen. Yes, *listen.* Shh ... Wait. Before your mind starts racing with all the times you have "held your tongue" with your ex when you really wanted to give her a piece of what she deserved, I want you to be silent. I know that your first response when someone asks you to *listen* is to convince them, and yourself, that you are a good listener; in fact, you are a better listener than your ex. You might be. You may be the best listener in the world, but when it comes to your relationship with your ex, I need you to be very attentive—not to her, but to *yourself.* So, with that direction, I want you to start with the assumption that we are all poor listeners, especially when we are frustrated or angry. We often ignore what we know— our long-term aspirations—because frustration and emotional charge get in the way of us really listening. I think that you would agree that divorce can be one of the most frustrating, most anger-provoking experiences out there, which makes staying calm and listening very challenging.

Anger and frustration are roadblocks to listening to others and ourselves. Even worse, when people feel justified in their positions or believe that they have been wronged, they have a hard time listening. Ask any customer service representative about how difficult it is to communicate with people who feel that they have been treated poorly! Interestingly, while the customer may be enraged about the company not listening, that same customer has fallen into the same non-listening trap. Communication stops. Now, multiply the reaction of the wronged customer by at least ten and that may reflect how *wronged* people often feel in their relationships with their exes. Do you feel wronged by your ex? Do you feel that no matter what you do or say, your ex uses it to his advantage? Do you feel that you have been victimized by your ex and that he is now using the entire legal system against you?

To determine your individual challenge to listening, I want you to consider the following statement. Circle the number that best represents how you would complete this sentence: *In my relationship with my ex, I feel that he treats me fairly …*

1-----2-----3-----4-----5-----6-----7-----8-----9-----10

Never   Sometimes   All of the time

You may feel that your ex never considers your needs. You may feel that this has improved over time, and sometimes he actually listens to you. If you are at the 9 or 10 mark, you are doing very well. As you can probably guess, the closer you are to the 1 rating, the more challenging it is to listen to someone who you feel treats you unfairly. Understandably, it is difficult to trust that what you say to someone who has wronged you in the past, or even on a consistent basis, will be accepted.

As I indicated, I am not expecting you to listen to your ex; that would just be a bonus to this entire process. My goal is for you to listen to yourself—what you know about what you want, and what you need to do for long-term gain. While you may have known that anger toward your ex makes it difficult for you to listen to him, you may not have considered that the closer you are to the 1 rating, the more difficult it is to listen to yourself. The anger needs to dissipate so that you can listen to yourself.

It's a good thing you know from previous chapters that you are in control of yourself. You're separated or divorced from your couple relationship. Your ex no longer has the power to make you behave in ways that are contrary to who you are as a person and a parent. Good thing you have complete control over your behavior, right?

In the previous chapters I asked you to think about yourself differently. You have considered your identity and your beliefs about what it means to be an ex-spouse when you have children. I am now asking you to think about how you can listen to yourself in order to meet your needs and those of your children. To listen is to support healing for yourself and your children.

So how do we define listen? First, listening requires silence. Yes, complete silence. No interjecting. No formulating a response in your head before the other person has finished speaking. When was the last time through this process of separation and divorce that you considered *silence* a tool to get what you need—what your kids need? When was the last time you considered silence to be a form of self-expression?

In the last chapter, I talked about taking a different position from one that wasn't working. I talked about shifting to thinking about long-term gain from defense mode. By understanding what divorce means for you, this shift is within reach. You will know that you've made this shift when you are able to *stop talking and listen.* Listen not just to what others are saying, but to your inner voice. Listen to what you know—your internal dialogue and your knowledge—before you respond to the situation at hand. Some parents I've worked with have asked me, "You want me to shut up and listen to myself?"

My response to them (and to you) is:

> *Yes. I say this in the most respectful manner. I want you to shut up, listen to what you've said, what you know now, and how you feel now. I want you to be silent unless you can logically convince yourself that saying something will make this situation better than it is currently. If you conclude that saying something will not improve the situation, your best strategy is to say nothing.*

I know this to be true and so do you. Remember all of those affidavits, e-mails, and letters that you threw out when you were ridding your environment to clear the path? Was all of that correspondence, coupled with the verbal exchange, working? Was it working for you? Was it working for your ex? I doubt it, because communicating with anyone in an emotionally charged manner is risky. The points we are most trying to convey get lost in the desire to make the other person hear you … to make the other person *understand* you. When the situation involves parenting with an ex, communicating in an emotionally charged manner is not only risky, it is also hazardous to your health.

Most of us have an intuitive need to behave so that others will like us—we want to be accepted. It is hard to understand why someone who by all accounts loved us enough to procreate now purposefully treats us badly. We convince ourselves that they must not understand what they are doing! We sometimes expect that if we just try harder, *make them listen,* they will see the error in their ways and be nicer to us. I hate to be the bearer of bad news, but this is regrettably not the case.

For the purpose of understanding, let's take the example away from one of divorce. Not so long ago a woman, Janet, came to my office appearing stressed and frustrated. She reported that she believed she was being bullied by her coworkers—people she had considered to be friends for several years. Over a nine-year period, Janet's career had advanced to the level of middle management. She felt proud of this accomplishment and described dedicated efforts to make the business flourish. She perceived this as a benefit to all who were employed by the company. Janet was responsible for a team of ten people, many of whom had joined the company during the same time period as her. Unfortunately, as all middle managers know, it is often a difficult role to be both in the trenches with the workforce while also being part of the management team. Over the past year, Janet felt that her subordinates, who were to report directly to her, were attempting to undermine her role. Specifically, they had been holding meetings without her, sending e-mails to her superiors, and failing to implement changes she directed. Further, perhaps most hurtful to Janet, was a decision seemingly made by the group to leave her out of the annual summer party that she had founded seven years ago in her own backyard! Janet was emotionally overwhelmed. She explained that she had come to me because she wanted her coworkers to *understand* how hurtful their behavior has been for her. She wanted her coworkers to *understand* that despite her role as a manager, she could still be their friend. She wanted to find a way to communicate her needs to her coworkers.

I listened to Janet, and I could hear the pain she was experiencing. Janet felt hurt, anger, and sadness because with this change in her life came losses. I understood her desire to alleviate this pain and heal the emotional wounds caused by these experiences.

Through therapy, I could help Janet learn to communicate better. I have expertise in communication and relationships—work relationships, intimate relationships, and friendships. However, Janet and I could have spent weeks perfecting her communication strategies. We could have held a group session with Janet and her team to focus on team-building. We could have done lots of things that we didn't do.

Why? Why did we not focus on supporting Janet in making her team understand her feelings? We didn't do any of these things because first we needed to change Janet's expectations. "Janet," I explained, "The problem is not that these people don't understand; the problem is that you are expecting them to care." When Janet first heard my words her posture changed. Her jaw tightened and her back straightened. I could see the hurt in her face—a reality check that people she once cared about no longer considered her worthy of their investment. Small tears pushed their way to the corner of her left eye and then rolled down her flushed cheek. She sighed, and, for a moment, I anticipated a defensive response, something like, "Of course they care about me, I …" Before any words came out, Janet paused, wiped the tears from her face, and nodded. "You know what?" she responded. "You're right."

Like you, Janet was under the false impression that by compelling the other person, or in Janet's case *people*, to *understand* what she was experiencing, they would change their behavior. Janet was neglecting to understand that when her role changed or sometime thereafter, people she was now managing stopped caring about how she felt or what she was experiencing. Janet and I took some time to reflect upon what may have altered these relationships but ultimately concluded that, quite simply, her change in role had *changed* how much others were willing to invest in *understanding* her needs, feelings, and experiences.

You may wonder why I have taken the time to tell you about Janet. After all, as far as you know, Janet isn't parenting after divorce.

First, I'm not telling you Janet's story because she agreed with me. I am telling you about Janet because, like you, Janet had to let go of the expectation that people she cared about, people who also once cared about her, no longer care enough to *understand* what she is going through. They really don't care that she feels left out, hurt, or disrespected by their behavior. If they did, they would not have left her out of an annual party that she founded! They absolutely don't care that she feels they are undermining her efforts. If they did, they would not send e-mails to her superiors. When Janet changed roles, her relationship with her former friends changed and so did their willingness to care about how she feels.

Sound familiar? Your role has changed. You are no longer a spouse to your child's other parent. You are an ex-spouse. With estrangement, particularly when accompanied by conflict, ex-spouses often come to a decision, whether consciously or unconsciously, to no longer care about what you are feeling. I promise that, like Janet, no matter how hard you try, even equipped with the most skilled techniques available in communication, if you try to make your ex *understand*, your efforts will be futile. On the other hand, he may already understand. When Janet's coworkers left her out of the annual party, they probably understood that this would be hurtful. When your ex made a snide comment to you in the parking lot or failed to share your child's school photos, he probably knew that would be hurtful. The problem is not lack of understanding. The problem is lack of caring. Your ex no longer cares to make your life better. When he was married to you, he probably made efforts to understand your needs and feelings because he cared. He no longer feels that obligation to you.

This is not a question of *should*. Yes, we should care about how our actions affect others. Yes, we should care very much when our actions hurt the parent of a child we love very much. We are responsible for how we behave. We may not care about our exes' feelings because we still love them, but we should care because it is in our best interests to care—financially, legally, and psychologically. When we behave in a way that considers how our exes may feel, we do ourselves a favor.

Nick, a successful accountant, had been divorced from Monique for eight years. It was by all descriptions a bitter divorce, with Monique engaging in an affair prior to their separation. Nick and Monique's three children were privy to the affair long before Nick. In fact, Nick's eldest child ultimately disclosed her knowledge about her mother's new boyfriend before Monique shared her new relationship with Nick. A litigious process followed. Nick moved out of the matrimonial home, and Monique's new boyfriend moved in with Monique. While the children initially stayed with Monique to avoid changing schools, following conflict between the eldest child and the new boyfriend, all three children moved to live primarily with Nick. Custody and financial disagreements followed for several years. Communication between Nick and Monique was largely nonexistent with the exception of rare exchanges that were unpleasant for both parties.

Four years after the final settlement, Nick began a relationship with another woman. From Nick's perspective, Monique took a negative position on this relationship and too often shared her unfiltered views with the children. Despite the children adapting positively to this new woman, Nick felt that Monique was most bothered by the younger age of his new girlfriend. One evening, following a busy after-school schedule of transporting the children from gymnastics, to music lessons, to tutoring for their middle child, Nick, his new girlfriend, and the children stopped at a local pizza restaurant for dinner.

The group entered the restaurant and followed the hostess to their table. As they progressed to their table, Nick heard his youngest child exclaim, "It's Mommy!" Nick glanced sideways to see Monique standing at the salad bar. Monique reached out to hug their child but her eyes were fixed on Nick and then his new girlfriend. Without hesitation, she commented, "Did you ask for four children's menus?"

In his session with me, Nick reported that he was furious with Monique's comment in the presence of the children. However, he stopped, thought about this response, and refocused his attention on his children. He purposefully looked at his three children— one standing next to Monique and the others uncomfortably standing next to him. His thoughts had raced, his cheeks felt flushed. How dare she? She was the one who had the affair. She was the one who threw their marriage away. He spends his life looking after their children. He was a good father. Did she have any idea of how he had spent the last three hours?

Then, taking a deep breath, Nick did himself a big favor. Nick reminded himself to *"shut up and listen. Listen to what I know. Listen to what I have learned."* Nick reminded himself that Monique's actions had nothing to do with him. Nick reminded himself that Monique was an intelligent person. She probably understood that by making that comment, Nick would feel anger and hurt. She likely understood that such a comment would not make Nick's life better. Heck, she probably even considered that he might not enjoy his dinner with the children if she upset him with such a comment. She did not care. Nick reminded himself of these things. In fact, he repeated them more than once. Then he sauntered to his table. He did not respond. In fact, not only did he not respond verbally, he stopped responding psychologically. Monique did not care about Nick, and Nick accepted this. Nick suggested that the children choose their favorite pizza off the menu and he began to enjoy dinner with his kids. Nick remained silent, listened to himself, and continued to remain silent. His children won. There is no better outcome than that.

So I've told you about Janet and Nick. Now it is your turn to listen to yourself. Take a few minutes to complete these exercises:

If it was up to me, I would want my ex to *understand* …

_____

_____

_____

_____

_____

I felt hurt by my ex when …

_____

_____

_____

_____

_____

I wish I hadn't responded when ...

_____

_____

_____

_____

Now that I understand that the problem is not lack of understanding on the part of my ex, I will ...

_____

_____

_____

_____

We are all human. We want people to hear us, understand us, and care about us. We inherently believe that if we make people understand, they will do the right thing. Unfortunately, as wars, terrorism, fraud, crime, and all things evil prove otherwise, we can't make people do the right thing. We can, however, choose not to participate in the wrong thing. In the case of conflict between ex-spouses, the wrong thing is to engage in unchecked, unfiltered self-expression where you say what you feel regardless of the consequences. I promise you—such behavior is contrary to your self-interest and the interest of your children. You know that you have control over your behavior, the ability to separate your feelings from your behavior, and the responsibility of being the best parent you can be in spite of your ex. The right thing is to focus on happiness, healing, and parenting—parenting apart in a child-focused way.

Let's Talk Money

One of my lawyer friends is certain that all conflict between ex-spouses can be traced back to disagreements about money. I believe that money is one source of tension after a relationship ends, but I also believe that money often masks the real problems in the relationship.

Arguments about money are symptomatic of the state of most divorced relationships. During and following divorce, people agree about few things and argue about many. These arguments are likely to resurface even when you are able to fully disengage from your ex. From media reports about astronomical lawsuits, you know that one way people show that they are unhappy or feel slighted is by demanding compensation for their suffering. While your ex may be asking for more money, or alternatively asking to pay less money, the demands may have more to do with his attributing his unhappiness to you. If it is you that is asking for more money or asking to pay less money, I want you to consider what is fueling this need. Is the issue purely financial?

I think if you review your responses to the exercises, you'll identify that what you have found frustrating in your relationship with your ex may relate to feeling undervalued or not valued at all. Similarly, if your ex completed a similar exercise, his response may indicate the same. You may also find that you are frustrated by the lack of progress in repairing the *parental* relationship between you and your ex. Until now, there may have been an expectation that your ex would "come to his senses" or "get on with his life," leaving the anger toward you behind. There may also have been an expectation that your ex would acknowledge his responsibility in this situation and start communicating with you differently. Given that you are still feeling frustrated, this probably hasn't happened. As you have progressed through these chapters, you now understand that this may *never* happen. With *understanding* you have the power to change … to change your expectations … to change your beliefs … to change what you do. With these changes, you will disengage from the conflict with your ex and allow yourself to parent *in spite of* the situation. When you prove to yourself that you can do this, you will not only be a better parent; you will also find joy in parenting after divorce. Is fighting over money a symptom of attaching a value to what you have been through, what you have continued to experience?

I talked about the importance of learning to *regulate*. Financial disputes or arguments over money are sometimes symptomatic of a lack of regulation. When people's fights about money involve lawyers and courts, one thing is for certain: everyone loses. Everyone, that is, except lawyers.

As I discussed in the beginning of this book, when people litigate family matters, common sense seems to go by the wayside. For example, by the time many separated people finish legally battling about assets and support payments, they have spent thousands of dollars to increase monthly payments only a couple of hundred dollars. Unless you are some sort of celebrity or billionaire, this is a lot of money for most people. Under normal, clear-thinking circumstances, very few people would agree to pay someone upwards of six hundred to eight hundred dollars per hour to help sort out a family problem. However, when emotions run high, normally fiscally-responsible, rational people do not even take pause when they retain a lawyer to battle their exes. Somehow as a society we have become convinced that it is reasonable to give up our life savings— our savings for our children—to end a marriage with a spouse. When lawyers quote clients astronomical fees, normally sane people say, "Okay, where do I sign?" This speaks to the divorce culture. The divorce industry is built upon people's inability to self-regulate and effectively control their behaviors and decision-making during what should be a family transition.

A transition from marriage to life after divorce has turned into an adversarial, extremely expensive process for parents and children. You do not need to be part of this process. Essentially, whatever money you are going to walk away with is a fraction of what you could have had simply by making the choice to disengage.

If you and your ex have disputed or are disputing finances, I would like you to tally how much you have spent to date.

The total amount I have spent on legal bills is:

_____

_____

_____

_____

_____

What do I anticipate that the cost will be to complete this process?

_____

_____

_____

_____

_____

How does the amount I have spent on legal bills affect the rest of my life?

_____

_____

_____

_____

Will the money that I have spent on legal bills be offset by what I will gain?

_____

_____

_____

If I decided to step out of the legal battle now, what would be the risk?

_____

_____

_____

If I decided to step out of the legal battle now, what would be the benefit to me?

_____

_____

_____

_____

When people approach financial decisions, they lose sight of important facts that can affect their lives on a long-term basis. We've all been there. Who hasn't purchased something, large or small, with the hope that it would make them *feel* better? When many of us made that purchase, the question of whether we could actually afford the item was not the first priority. Instead, we asked whether we deserved the item or whether it would feel good to have the item.

Ask the millions of shoppers with credit card debt how an emotional approach to making financial decisions is working for them.

Divorce, as I have discussed, can be highly emotional. People who usually approach challenges or problems pragmatically make emotionally-based decisions. By completing the above exercise, you have taken the time to financially consider how your decision-making is impacting your bank account and your financial stability. Accounting decisions should not be addressed emotionally. If you don't have the money to take on or continue a legal battle, approach the issue with an accounting lens. Take emotion out of decisions that involve money!

Chapter 6

Here Comes the Sun, It's All Right

You've almost reached your destination. You've visualized it. You've taken the necessary steps to achieve it. Now you are ready to embrace it. Dynamic disengagement—the place where divorced parents are free from the stress and frustration brought on by a contentious relationship with their ex-spouses. It's just around the next bend. The weight you have been carrying for months, maybe years, will be taken off your shoulders. The best news is that it's not just a vacation destination (where you take a break from your ex); it is a *life destination*. This is the place you will truly live from this point forward, the place where you focus on you, your child, and happiness. Gone are the days when your happiness is overshadowed by the contempt of your ex. You have cleared the path, navigated the relationship by learning to regulate your feelings and behaviors, and have accepted full responsibility for your happiness.

You are preparing to arrive at your destination. Make sure you have all of your belongings. Make sure that you have reviewed the strategies and practiced them with your ex and with others in your life. Remain conscious of your feelings and, more importantly, your behaviors. You have learned that if you are to live a happy life, disengaged from the conflict with your ex, your feelings cannot direct your behavior! How you behave with your ex—the other parent of your child—must be an intellectual decision, not emotional.

To achieve dynamic disengagement, you have executed four key strategies. You will need to remain conscious of these strategies to sustain the changes you have made.

Remember, your ex has not changed and will continue to behave in a manner that has upset you in the past. The only thing that you have control over is your response. When behaviors are thrown at you by your ex, you must stop and listen to what you already know. As the fireman taught you to stop, drop and roll, you must consciously:

1. Understand;
2. Choose your Path;
3. Regulate to Navigate;
4. Self-Attribute.

When you choose your path, remind yourself that you are driving your own bus. Your ex can drive his bus of conflict off a cliff, but you aren't going with him. Your ex can choose to veer into a traffic jam of unhappiness, but you already know your route. Your path heads to dynamic disengagement, regardless of the scenario. Regardless of the issue he is unhappy about, your response is predetermined. You will remain silent unless you can rationally conclude that saying or doing something will improve the situation. You have learned to regulate your behaviors because you understand that your ex really doesn't care what you think or how you feel, and therefore you are not going to waste energy and risk your happiness in an effort to convince him to do the right thing. You are simply going to do the right thing for your happiness and that of your child. You follow this script, this route, and this plan consistently because you understand that you, and you alone, are responsible for your happiness. You do not attribute your unhappiness to others. No one, not even your ex, has this power over you.

When we truly understand self-attribution, or personal responsibility for our lives, we accept that how we manage our emotions has nothing to do with how others manage theirs. In fact, when others show lack of regulation, our ability to regulate should increase as we become conscious of this need.

I would like you to refer back to the My Profile you created on page 29. Remember when you listed all of the statements that you had answered yes to? Those statements are strengths. In this section, I am asking you to only identify the statements that you answered no to. For example, if you circled no to 11) *I am part of a larger community,* list that statement on the lines below. When you are finished listing all of the no statements, take a moment and read them back to yourself.

_____

_____

_____

_____

_____

_____

_____

_____

_____

You may be thinking, *I don't have time for this self-care crap! I've got stuff to take care of. My ex is probably devising another scheme right now to wreck my life!* You are afraid to shift out of defense mode. You want to be ready for whatever comes—in the mail, by phone, by text. You may feel that if you let your defenses down, you are going to get hit. I'm telling you that if you don't shift from your defense mode, forget getting hit; you are going to get sick ... sick emotionally ... sick financially ... maybe sick physically ... definitely sick of this situation. You need to understand the *long-term benefit* of doing things differently.

The statements that you have written above are those that did not make it to your yes list. They are not yet able to help fuel you through this difficult time. The good news? With action, they will! Can you think of one of those statements that you would like to move to your yes list? Start there. Whenever you feel overwhelmed by a challenge or a situation, it is important to stop, think, and break it down into manageable tasks. Choose one of the statements from your list of no statements and write it below:

_____

_____

_____

_____

_____

_____

_____

_____

Now no longer is this a *no* statement but rather a goal statement. Think of it as the next statement that will fuel your *yes* list. The more statements on your yes list, the better you will feel about yourself and your situation. I am asking you to look at the rest of your life, your work, your family, and your friends because your life as a parent does not occur in isolation from the rest of your world. When we examine our feelings and behaviors, and we seek to understand the behaviors of others (such as our ex-spouses), we must consider that people do not behave or feel a certain way because of one thing. Our behaviors and feelings are influenced by *many* things in our lives.

Let's look at another relevant example. Max was a forty-four-year-old father of three children, ranging in age from seven through twelve years. His ex-wife Laura travelled extensively in her work as a freelance writer. Her schedule was often unpredictable and, largely for financial reasons, Max decided to accommodate Laura's request for a flexible parenting plan whereby the children were with her when she was at home and with Max during periods when she was required to travel. Initially, Max was happy with this arrangement. Laura had a very busy year following their separation, requiring her to be away from home up to nineteen days per month. However, into the second year of the agreement, the economy suffered a downturn and consequently Laura's client list decreased. As a result, Laura was only away from home approximately ten to twelve days per month. Laura and Max communicated relatively well until Laura began demanding more time with the children. Max acknowledged that he resented his time with the children being decreased due to Laura's increased downtime from work, and Laura reported that she could feel Max's hostility in their communication. Laura knew that Max was upset by having less time with the children but felt that he agreed to this plan and it was her turn to benefit. She was frustrated by his selfishness and felt he should understand how important it was for the children to have time with her when, at any time, her traveling commitments could increase again. Max felt that Laura should understand what a drastic change he and the children were experiencing by being forced to accommodate Laura's schedule. When they arrived at my office, the parents had attended two sessions of mediation but felt deadlocked. Max threatened that he was going to take the matter before the court, and Laura threatened that if he did so, she would pursue sole custody, as they clearly were unable to communicate (inability to communicate is often a key factor judges cite when making awards of sole custody).

Max and Laura presented with symptoms of anger, frustration, intolerance, and fatigue. Neither really wanted to go to court. As many divorced parents do, the threat of court is used in an attempt to force the other parent to agree with his or her position. It is a poor strategy and rarely effective. You see, it is not simply that they did not understand the position of the other parent. Max understood that Laura wanted more time with their children; Laura understood that Max wanted the same. *Understanding* was not the problem. The problem was *expectations*. As long as you, or any divorced parent, expect that the other parent is going to value your position over his own, you will be disappointed. Except in rare cases, this never happens. When a point of conflict ensues, even in good post-divorce parenting relationships, you must enter any communication with the *understanding* that you are not going to shift the position of the other parent. He may "get" where you are coming from, but he will act only from his own position.

So how do people like Max and Laura resolve matters of disagreement? First, they must expect that if the matter is left to the court, it will not turn out well for a variety of reasons. Number

1: It is costly. Court action will deplete savings and spend money that you have not even made yet. You can lose your house and your savings, and some have lost jobs, all in an effort to keep the legal wheels turning. The lawyers will benefit; you and your kids will lose. Number 2: A stranger will decide how you are going to live your life after divorce. The stranger, otherwise known as a judge, will do her best to make a decision, but she doesn't know you, hasn't met your kids, and has probably been jaded by years of dealing with people just like you and your ex taking up court time and resources. Number 3: It sends the wrong message to your kids. By throwing decision-making to a stranger, you and your ex are telling your kids that you aren't even capable of making decisions about the most important thing in your lives—them. Bottom line? Stop threatening court. Stop responding to threats about court. If your ex brings court up, tell him that you have no control over his decisions, but court action alone shows an inability to be child-focused. Then leave it. If you receive a letter from his lawyer, use a response of disengagement. Do not fuel the fire by pouring more allegations onto paper. If you are required to obtain a lawyer, ensure that your select counsel understands that your goal is to disengage and not inflame the situation. Therefore, there are no inflammatory letters from counsel, no threats of sole custody—just a desire to settle amicably. Finally, understand that divorce court is not service-oriented. It is not the judge's responsibility to make the process user friendly. It is a challenging, exhausting place and process.

Max and Laura finally agreed that under no circumstances would they threaten one another with further court action. They recalled how during their marriage they had adhered to a "no threat of divorce" policy during arguments. Like rules of fair fighting during marriage, they were willing to follow a fair-fighting policy during separation. What are the rules of communicating with an ex?

As Max and Laura found, the greatest skill is being able to walk away—to disengage. They realized that while there is no handbook for being in a parenting relationship with an ex, there are rules of engagement that apply to any conflict. Be polite. Be respectful. Don't set up unfair expectations because you will only be disappointed. Finally, realize that there are no winners in divorce, and it is more important to be content than to be right.

Now it's your turn. Using the knowledge and strategies discussed in these chapters, it is your turn to create your own customized life plan. This plan begins with the premise that your ex is not going to help you make life better. In fact, he has proven that he will do everything within his reach to make life difficult. In the final section of this book, I have provided a concise 28-day workbook to detox from your old behavior and embrace new, healthy coping strategies. Get your life back! The only tools you need are a pen and some quiet space. The workbook is the place to direct all of the feelings you would normally direct at your ex—your feelings about you and your kids and how you feel about life after divorce. I have provided one sentence per day to get you started, but do not limit yourself to completing only one sentence. The days rotate between thinking days and action days. This will keep you motivated to do things differently! Let your feelings out on paper—not in your response to your ex!

Your 28-Day Plan

Week One: 7-Day Ex Detox

Day 1: Think!

Today I will consider all things that I am happy

about in my new life as a divorced person. This is

a "take notice" exercise. As I go about my day, I

will choose to shine the spotlight on all things that

are positive and good.

Consciously deciding to look at the positives made me feel ...

_____

_____

_____

_____

_____

_____

_____

_____

_____

_____

_____

_____

_____

_____

_____

_____

_____

Day 2: Action!

> *Today I will rid my home of the things that keep me trapped in the toxic dynamics with my ex. Time to rip, shred, or erase triggers and memories of conflict! (Note: You may have already completed this step while you were reading the book. If so, use this action day as an opportunity to choose a positive activity for yourself, like a walk on the beach, having coffee with a neighbor, or heading to the park with your kids).*

Getting rid of the affidavits, letters, e-mails, and texts made me feel …

_____

_____

_____

or

Taking time to create positive energy made me feel …

_____

_____

_____

Day 3: Think!

> *Today I will be thoughtful of the positive, healthy relationships in my life. I will notice healthy people in my life who, until now, I have not considered as people of importance. I will remember that I have the power to surround myself with good people.*

I felt surprised by ...

_____

_____

_____

_____

_____

_____

_____

_____

_____

_____

_____

_____

_____

Day 4: Action!

Today I will write a letter to my ex. (Not to share with your ex. Remember, this is for your benefit, not to inflame the situation). I will tell my ex how his actions have made me feel. At the end of the letter, I will tell my ex that he/she no longer has power over me. I will remember that I have the power to decide who will not be part of my inner circle.

Dear ...

_____

_____

_____

_____

_____

_____

_____

_____

_____

_____

_____

_____

Day 5: Think!

> *Today I will take time to visualize my future as*
> *a happy, divorced person. I will contemplate how*
> *being free from my ex will change how I live day*
> *to day.*

If I didn't spend time thinking about my ex, I would have time
to …

_____

_____

_____

_____

_____

_____

_____

_____

_____

_____

_____

_____

_____

_____

_____

Day 6: Action!

Today I will reach out to a friend. I will tell my friend that I am moving on with my life and that I realize I am responsible for my happiness. By telling someone close to me about my journey, I am reaching out for support and building a support system of people that I can trust.

Reaching out to a friend made me feel ...

_____

_____

_____

_____

_____

_____

_____

_____

_____

_____

_____

_____

_____

_____

Day 7: Think!

> *I'm proud of myself! Today I will identify the positive changes I have made in my life since my marriage/relationship ended. Am I a more involved parent? Do I feel calmer in my home?*

The positive changes I have made have made me feel ...

_____

_____

_____

_____

_____

_____

_____

_____

_____

_____

_____

_____

_____

_____

_____

_____

_____

Congratulations!

You've finished Week One! Now it's time to create building blocks for success!

Week Two: Creating New Behaviors and
Securing Health and Happiness

Day 8: Action!

Today I will review my finances and create a rational plan for my future. I will consider the financial changes that have occurred since my separation as well as the court/legal costs to date. If needed, I will enlist the help of a financial advisor.

By dealing with the reality of my financial situation, I have achieved ...

_____

_____

_____

_____

_____

_____

_____

_____

_____

_____

Day 9: Think!

> *Today I will identify three goals for the future. My goals will be attainable. As a suggestion, one goal may relate to finances, one goal to personal relationships, and one goal to health (physical and/or emotional). Each goal must be measureable (how will I know when I have achieved this goal?) and action-oriented (I will ...).*

My goals for the next year ...

_____

_____

_____

_____

_____

_____

_____

_____

_____

_____

_____

_____

Day 10: Action!

> *Today I will take action on one of my goals. For example, if my goal is to be in better physical health, I will take a walk on my lunch break. If my goal is to spend more time with my children, I will put away my laptop and get out a board game.*

By taking action, I benefitted by ...

_____

_____

_____

_____

_____

_____

_____

_____

_____

_____

_____

_____

_____

_____

_____

Day 11: Think!

> *Today I will make a list of what is within my con-*
> *trol. As I have been focusing more on me and my*
> *children, I have noticed that my ex is taking up*
> *less space in my head. This feels great! I need to*
> *remind myself of how magnificent it feels to be in*
> *control of my life!*

Wow! When I think about what is within my control, I feel ...

_____

_____

_____

_____

_____

_____

_____

_____

_____

_____

_____

_____

_____

Day 12: Action!

> *Today I will take action on my second goal. One*
> *step forward, just like the other day. Remember,*
> *Rome wasn't built in a day and neither are lives*
> *after divorce!*

Taking action on my second goal is an accomplishment. It makes me feel ...

_____

_____

_____

_____

_____

_____

_____

_____

_____

_____

_____

_____

Day 13: Think!

> *Today I will take time to reflect on what I have learned from my separation/divorce (other than your ex is a ****!). From the most difficult experiences comes the most valuable learning. Use this experience as something that enriched your life rather than something that eroded it. Remember you are in control. Make this experience work for your life after divorce rather than against it!*

While this has been a hellish experience, I am walking out of the flames. I will never go back. Although not unscathed, I choose to take from this experience …

_____

_____

_____

_____

_____

_____

_____

_____

Day 14: Action!

> *Today I will apply my learning to my new life. I will be a good listener and a support to someone who needs it. Support may come in the form of a smile, a random act of kindness, or reaching out to a friend or an acquaintance who is going through a difficult time.*

When I gave support to someone in need, I felt ...

_____

_____

_____

_____

_____

_____

_____

_____

_____

_____

_____

_____

_____

_____

_____

_____

Dr. Julie Gowthorpe, R.S.W.

Congratulations!

You have completed Week Two! Your sense of self is secure, and you are confident in your ability to disengage from your ex. You are ready to progress to responding to your ex differently than you have ever done before! Because you cannot control when or how your ex will behave badly, or on what days your children are with you, you are in control of how you complete the next twelve days. When you complete a Think or Action exercise, simply check off that day. Because of factors outside of your control, it is not necessary that you complete the days in chronological order.

Day 15: Think!

> *Today I will review my building blocks. How have*
> *I re-established control over my life? How have*
> *I filled my life with positive energy from people I*
> *choose to allow into my inner circle?*

I have changed my lens on how I view life. I now see my future differently because ...

_____

_____

_____

_____

_____

_____

_____

_____

_____

_____

_____

_____

Day 16: Action!

> *Today when my ex sends me a nasty text or e-mail with a tone that is negative, I will simply not respond. If it involves scheduling something for the children, I will respond only with basic information (time and/or date and/or location) and finish with a "thanks." Remember, your ex wants to fight with you, but you are stepping out of the ring. Your ex does not have the power to control you.*

By not engaging in the negative exchange with my ex, I was empowered because ...

_____

_____

_____

_____

_____

_____

_____

_____

_____

_____

Day 17: Think!

> *Today I will consider the stressors that have influenced how I cope with my ex. I will also consider the stressors that my ex may be dealing with— not because I need to feel bad for my ex, but because it is in my self-interest to not take his behavior personally.*

Stressors that I am dealing with include ...

_____

_____

_____

_____

_____

It's not about me. Some stressors that my ex is dealing with may include ...

_____

_____

_____

_____

_____

_____

_____

_____

Day 18: Action!

> *Today when I am with my kids, I will be aware that they have one world. I will show interest in the time they spend with my ex, and reinforce him as a parent by making at least one positive comment. This will demonstrate to my kids that I am okay with their love for my ex.*

When I made a positive comment about my ex, I noticed that my kids ...

_____

_____

_____

_____

_____

_____

_____

_____

_____

_____

Day 19: Think!

Today I will focus on what I love about being a divorced parent. For example, "I am able to have time with my child that is not marred by the tension between me and my ex. How I manage my time with my child is my responsibility and that feels great!"

By focusing on the positive aspects of being a divorced parent, I noticed ...

_____

_____

_____

_____

_____

_____

_____

_____

_____

_____

Day 20: Action!

Today I will make a conscious, purposeful decision to not respond to my ex when I feel that he criticizes me as a parent. While I recognize that I may feel defensive or hurt when he questions my capabilities or investment in my children, I realize that it is in my self-interest to remain silent. It's not about me—it's about his inability to disengage.

When I did not respond to my ex, I felt empowered because I have achieved disengagement. Regardless of my ex's behavior, I am confident that I ...

_____

_____

_____

_____

_____

_____

_____

_____

_____

_____

Day 21: Think!

> *Today I will take notice of the things I cannot*
> *change. I will accept the things that I cannot*
> *change (like my ex's anger toward me) because I*
> *am then empowered to minimize the impact upon*
> *my life. I am a tank of positive energy. I will not*
> *allow negative things to deplete my positive re-*
> *serve.*

When I direct my energy to those things that fuel me (like my kids, my friends, my exercise routine), I am recharged. This makes me feel ...

_____

_____

_____

_____

_____

_____

_____

_____

_____

_____

Dr. Julie Gowthorpe, R.S.W.

Day 22: Action!

> _Today I will revisit my no statements from My Profile on page 29. I will review whether changes have occurred and select one no statement (for example, "I have good physical health") that continues to require my attention. I will use my journaling activity for the day to map out an action plan._

My action plan to change my no statement of (for example, _"I have good physical health"_) is ...

_____

_____

_____

_____

_____

_____

_____

_____

_____

_____

100

Day 23: Think!

> *Today I will write a letter to my kids (but not to*
> *share with them) to express my feelings about*
> *what it means to be a parent. I will use this op-*
> *portunity to identify my strengths and areas that I*
> *would like to improve.*

Dear (names of child or children),

_____

_____

_____

_____

_____

_____

_____

_____

_____

_____

Day 24: Action!

> *Today I will implement the action plan I created on Day 22. I realize that this is one step toward being the happiest divorced person I can be. I do not expect to attain perfection in one day. This is a work in progress, and once I complete this action plan, I am committed to revisiting My Profile and no statements as needed.*

Implementing my action plan made me feel ...

_____

_____

_____

_____

_____

_____

_____

_____

_____

Day 25: Think!

> *Today I will pause and think, "What's better?"*
> *Each day I am one step closer to living my life*
> *after divorce in my own way. What is better since*
> *I separated from my ex?*

When I look back on the time since I separated from my ex, I know that I have created many good things. I know that I am better because ...

_____

_____

_____

_____

_____

_____

_____

_____

_____

_____

Day 26: Action!

> *Today I will share my feelings with people in my life that I care about. I will show thanks to those who have supported me through this time of transition and feel gratitude for those who have shown understanding. I do not expect a response from them, as my action is my own. I am pleased with my action regardless of their response.*

When I shared my gratitude with ...

I felt ...

_____

_____

_____

_____

_____

_____

_____

_____

_____

_____

Congratulations!

You have completed 26 days of the *Get Your Life Back Plan.* You are now in the final stretch—Review and Reward!

Day 27: Think!

> *Today I will review my progress. Have I remained silent when I wanted to lash out at my ex? Have I focused my energy on the positive things in my life rather than on my ex's attempts to create unhappiness for me? How have my new efforts benefitted me and my children?*

When I review my progress, I can identify changes that include ...

_____

_____

_____

_____

_____

_____

_____

_____

_____

Day 28: Action!

> *Today I will celebrate! I will smile at my ex (if I am in contact with him); I will smile when I engage in an activity and my ex is not clouding my thinking; I will smile when I am able to focus on my work rather than legal proceedings; I will smile with my children. I will look in the mirror and congratulate this happy, divorced person who is looking back at me. My celebration will continue for the rest of my life, because that is where my focus is— not divorce, but life itself.*

My life is one to celebrate because …

_____

_____

_____

_____

_____

_____

_____

_____

_____

Epilogue

Tainted Love: Now I Run from You

Your ex has put you through hell. Your ex has made your life miserable. I get it. Other people in similar situations also get it. When our exes refuse to let us move on, we dream of taking off—leaving them behind for happier places. Sounds appealing, right? When you experience an ex from hell, it seems like the best option may just be to run away. Unfortunately, with kids, a home, and a career, running is only a solution in your dreams. That's why you put the work into this program. Congratulations!

As you worked your way through the pages of this book, you developed an understanding of why it no longer matters if your ex is miserable. You have learned that your ex may be unhappy because he is still trying to stay connected with you or because he does not know how to redefine his role as a parent in the absence of having a couple relationship with you. Perhaps your ex is still grieving the loss of your relationship. More importantly, you have learned that knowing *why* can help you understand *how* you are going to do things differently. By acquiring knowledge and taking action, you now know that you no longer have to wait for your ex to move on for things to get better. A better life after divorce begins with you.

Now that you've completed the 28-Day *Get Your Life Back Plan*, you have psychologically left your ex behind. You cannot leave physically because you share children; however, to your ex, it may feel like you've run away, like you're avoiding or ignoring him. That's fine. Your ex may even try harder to get you to engage in very negative ways. You may experience an influx of negative messages, threatening legal correspondence, or more mixed messages in an effort to confuse you. It doesn't matter. Those manipulative strategies belong to your ex. You have your own strategies. Your strategies are rooted in research and clinical experience, and they all come down to one word: disengage. You're done with your ex's antics. See you later, ex!

Now what? Now you get to live your life. What's the best news? You didn't even have to run.

All the best.

CPSIA information can be obtained at www.ICGtesting.com
Printed in the USA
LVOW060856090812

293538LV00002B/2/P